Dad Differently: Babies

An Emotional Guide to the First Year of Parenting for the Modern Father

Dad Differently
Book 2

Adam Fletcher

Wanderlust Words

Why This Book Exists

If you're reading this, it's likely two monumental things have happened in your life:

1. You've just had a baby.
2. A friend or confused enemy bought you *Dad Differently: Pregnancy and Birth* <u>and</u> this book as a gift.

In any case, welcome. And if you've already read the first book in the series, welcome back. A brief reminder of why these books exist.

Three years ago, I was a father-to-be. My days passed in an anxious fog. I was a mess of contradictions. I wanted to nest. I wanted to run away to Siberia and rustle elk. I wanted to research everything. I wanted to forget it was happening.

To help me through this difficult period, friends bought me fatherhood books, ostensibly like this one but with titles along the lines of SUPER-FATHER-HEROMAN. These books presented fatherhood as a series of hackable challenges, often in checklist form.

Logistics. Fatherhood was all logistics.

But it wasn't logistics keeping me up at night. I had YouTube tutorials to teach me brilliant diaper-folding hacks and how to install car seats. No, I was struggling with the inside, hard-to-reach parts of becoming a father: thoughts, feelings, fears, and emotions.

I never found a book that helped with that, so I promised myself that once my daughter turned two and I had more time, I'd write the one I'd needed. It grew into a series. This is book two, which will guide you from the hospital through the whole amazing/terrifying first year.

I hope it helps.

Adam

PS While my goal isn't to exclude anyone, the focus of this book is on heterosexual parenting couples. More should be written about other family and parenting constellations, but I'm not the person to write it. You'll also notice a bias towards couples who have just had their first child because that's when they're most likely to be gifted these books, and when anxiety and excitement are at their highest.

PSS This book is comprised of personal anecdotes from my life in first person, using the pronoun *I*. There are also many entries that address the reader directly, in second-person, *You*. This allows me to explore common parenting issues that are common but weren't necessary a part of my family life. To be more broadly applicable, sometimes the gender of the babies in these entries are male, sometimes female. I intended to have a system with that but it broke down at some point and has not proved repairable, mostly because of my crippling laziness. Sorry.

Part One
The First Few Weeks
- Learner Parents

The Fourth Trimester

We left the hospital with an entire human more than we'd arrived with, which everyone was rather blasé about, I felt. Sitting in the back of the taxi, I felt a swarm of bees buzzing in my chest. My partner, Evelyn, and I were parents. We were in charge, sort of, kind of, I suppose, mostly.

The taxi pulled up in front of our apartment building. "Sorry she cried the whole way," I said to the driver. "Don't take it personally."

I reached round and removed Runa's belt, slid her car seat out, and lowered her onto the pavement. Evelyn wobbled off towards the door of the building.

A bike whizzed towards us.

HAZARD! I screamed, in my mind, jumping to protect our newborn, even though the bike was on the other side of the road and was actually being ridden really slowly by a child of, perhaps, seven.

"You'll get used to it," the taxi driver said, having come round to collect his money.

"To what?" I asked.

"All of it."

Vague, I said quietly, in my mind, as I scooped Runa up, groaning under the weight of her baby carrier, which, despite being 1 percent of its size somehow weighed 75 percent of a Land Rover Discovery.

I pointed up at our building. "This is it," I said, unnecessarily, because Runa was asleep. Again. "This is your home. Well, I mean, we rent it. All property is theft—that's what Marx believed. The real kicker is that they stole it all before you and I were born. We'll get to Marx a bit later in your training. After lunch, maybe."

I pushed on the door, which should have needed a key but didn't because it had been broken for months because all landlords are evil. We walked (well, I did) to the stairs.

HAZARD! I screamed, in my mind, as I gripped the handrail.

I overtook Evelyn, who was bent over and wheezing, on the second-floor landing. "Everything hurts," she said, as I passed. I could have waited, I suppose, but I was keen for Runa to begin her education. Due to some complications that had kept us at the hospital, she was nearly a week old; we'd wasted so much time. I hoped that by her third birthday, if we had to, or if on-rushing dystopia demanded it, we'd be able to cut her loose, crossbow in one tiny hand, encyclopaedia of wild edible mushrooms in the other, backpack full of bitcoin on her back.

Once in our flat, I carried her straight out to the balcony, where I had grown, lovingly and from just seeds, a variety of flowers I didn't know the names of. "Flowers," I said. "Bees fuck them. It's less weird than it sounds."

Runa didn't look at the flowers. I clicked in front of her eyes. She didn't open her eyes. She rarely opened her eyes. I took her tiny hand and rubbed it on the petals of a flower.

Which flower? Who knows.

"Red flower," I said, before remembering that she didn't

know the colour red, couldn't see the colour red, or see at all, really. Also, that she didn't understand human words yet.

"Enough flowers," I said, and carried her back inside. "Table," I said, while looking at a table. "Useful for performing ad hoc surgeries and eating lasagne."

I turned a few degrees. "Chair. Useful for smashing over the heads of your enemies." I turned a few more degrees. "Coffee table. Useful for smashing over the heads of your enemies and holding your coffee."

"Coffee," I said, even though there was no coffee around, so she'd have to take my word for its existence, although I suppose the fact we'd named a table after it was a big clue. "Gives you the strength to smash things over the heads of your enemies. It also makes you poop, which can be useful. Although not for you—you poop all the goddamn time. I've been meaning to have a word with you about that, actually. I'll put in on the agenda for the first family meeting." I sniffed. "Oh, you've pooped again, you little bugger. I just changed you as well. *Ugh.*"

I heard the toilet flush. Evelyn walked into the living room and draped herself across the couch, fluffing many of its pillows to reenact her favoured pregnancy pose: *Defeated Damsel.* You can take the baby out of the belly, but you can't take the belly out of the… Oh, no, that doesn't work.

"Can you bring her over here for a cuddle, please?" Evelyn asked.

"She's pooped."

Her nose turned up. "You do poops."

"I do poops."

"Bring her for a cuddle after then."

"A cuddle?" I spluttered. "How will that help our tiny wolf child?" Runa's hands thrashed. "That's good, baby," I said. "The thrashing. Keep thrashing." I looked down at her mother. "She doesn't seem interested in anything?"

"What did you expect?" Evelyn asked, as if it weren't obvious that I'd expected Runa to be interested in things, e.g. mysterious red flowers.

"Have you heard of the fourth trimester?" she asked.

"You know me well enough to know the answer to that."

"No," she said. "The answer is no." She brightened, which she did when know-all-ing. "Well, apparently, the correct gestation period is more like twelve months. Babies come out early. Which is why they're so useless."

"Oh," I said. "So, it's too early for training?"

"Yes," she said. "But never too early for an iced coffee."

"For Runa?"

"For me."

"Ah." I looked down at our daughter, content in the nook between my arm and chest, weighing about as much as a tin of baked beans. "Okay, sweet cheeks, first we're going to hit up the Nappy Changing Station. I think you're going to really appreciate the setup in there. I worked hard on it. Then we'll move on to the kitchen, where there are many weapons you can—"

"She comes here," Evelyn said. "De-pooped. She has no enemies—unlike you, if you don't bring me an iced coffee."

Now that you have a baby, it will be obvious to you she has entered the world early and undercooked. Humans should really have a longer gestation period, but as we covered in book one, once we stood upright, the birth canal became too narrow for our massive heads.

So, your baby is out, just about, but also, well, not really. The best thing you can do for her, beyond nappy changes (more on that later), is to care for her mother and create a variety of womb-like environments (that's what all the swaddling is about), to convince her that she's back inside the place she just left.

That's what she likes. That's what will make her both relax and sleep, which will make it possible for both you and your partner to relax and sleep. That's the fourth trimester, pretty much. When it's over, it's time to get out the nunchucks.

The Golden Hello

In any movie featuring a wedding, there's an obligatory honeymoon scene in which the couple wake up in bed together. The husband (let's call him Mr Stock Character) turns to his new bride. "Good morning, *Mrs* Stock Character," he says.

For some reason, she is in full makeup. Head against the pillow, she looks up, blinking several times, and smiles. "Why yes, it is a good morning, *Mr* Stock Character."

"What should we do today, *Mrs* Stock Character?"

"I can think of a few things," she says, and winks.

The audience gets the hint and prepares to leave, but there's still time for one last "Oh, can you now, *Mrs* Stock Character?"

They kiss.

Cut.

It's a lot of fun, that scene. We get the couple's excitement and understand that something fundamental has changed between them. They are now a team. A unit—*unit*ed in name.

Becoming parents is even more exciting because you *both* get new names. You live that same scene, knowing something fundamental has changed between you. That you are now a team, too. A unit: *Mum and Dad*.

There are stressors in the first weeks (breastfeeding is the big one, and we'll get to that later), but it's also a magical time; a Golden Hello to family life.

"Watermelon, *Mum*?" you ask, as you get up to go to the kitchen.

"Of course, *Dad*," she says.

You return with two plates and jolt with joy when you see that there's a whole extra human in the living room. Your human. A collage. Her nose. Your eyes. As for the rest? Let's see.

Mum is lying on her back, knees up. She's propped the baby against them, head supported by her thighs. "Look," she says, manoeuvring your newborn's arms back and forth, "two days old and already dancing."

"Arrrr," you say, as you put down the plates and search for your phone. It's only 9am but you've already recorded two hours of footage. Your WhatsApp has more ping-pong than the Beijing Olympics. You can't resist. You want to capture every moment of the Golden Hello.

"Do it again, *Mum*," you say, as you press record.

Mr Noboobs

In the first weeks of the fourth trimester, your newborn isn't an onion: he doesn't have layers. He is a simple, sucking thing; a mammal. In the few hours he is awake, he has only one hobby, interest, desire, and passion: milk.

He lives for milk.

He lives because of milk.

Which is a problem, assuming you and your partner have decided to breastfeed, since you don't have any boobs, do you? While this has made you, historically, motivated to go out and secure access to boobs, now, it makes you about as useful as a wet fart in a thunderstorm.

Or that's how it feels, anyway, as you watch your partner, depleted of life force, moaning in nipple-bleeding agony as your newborn, with his serious substance-abuse problem— off his tits on tits—refuse to get off the breast and go sleep it off, like the last drunk at the bra.

You try to wrench him away. "One more," he cries, raising his tiny index finger.

"Enough," you say, tugging him towards his cot.

His lip quivers and his head tips to the side and then

forwards. His eyes open and close and then snap awake. "DOUBLE. I'll take a double D."

"No, kid. Enough."

He looks at you with disgust. *Why are you even here? You are nothing. You are no one. Merely him with the proddy hands. Changer of nappy. Off-key song singer. Mr Noboobs.*

It hurts you, that look. Watching your newborn cuddle with your partner, seeing how much skin-to-skin action there is, seeing how much better Mama is at calming him when he cries, you might even believe you are unimportant. That the Divide, so prominent during pregnancy, has reopened.

It hasn't.

Breastfeeding is a full-time job. Which means your job is everything else. All of it—cooking, cleaning, shopping, walking the baby around, taking him out in the pram, cuddling, changing nappies, bathing, rocking him to sleep, cooking again, cleaning some more. Your partner, incapacitated for so much of the day, needs you more than ever. Your task list is full.

You are involved.

You are important.

You are Mr Noboobs, but Mr Noboobs matters.

The Nappy Change

I lowered Runa gently onto the changing mat in her room.

"Looking good, kid," I said, and clicked both hands. "Looking fresh, looking sharp. That tiny face." I stroked the cheek of that tiny face. "Hell of a face, that. Partly my face. Not that I'm bragging. Maybe I'm bragging. Anyway, let's get you a new nappy on and then it's straight back out to slay hearts and win minds. Maybe the other way round? I don't know. I'm sort of making this up as I go along. Can you tell?"

The biggest surprise of the first few weeks was just how much I loved the nappy changes. There had been so many, around ten a day, that by day three I knew what I was doing. And more than that, I liked what I was doing. Because here, away from the prying, preening, patronising eyes of her mother, Runa was all mine.

It was the Papa Show and I was proving—through songs, impressions, jokes, and bad dancing—that I was more than just Mr Noboobs.

I yanked a nappy from the pack and adopted a fairground-announcer voice. "Keep your hands inside the mat at all times, and scream if you want to be changed faster." Her head rolled to the side. I grabbed her feet and blew raspberries on their soles.

I had smelt poop, that was why we were here, that was what I was expecting, why I was already breathing through my mouth. Carefully, my movements full of loving grace, I popped each button on her romper and hoisted it up over her belly. Then I unfastened her nappy, holding her legs nice and high.

No poop, just a little wee.

"Ooooooh, baby, I love your wee," I sang, skilfully adapting a reggae classic.

Her eyes opened briefly and partially before closing again. A song came to me all at once and, elbows poking, hips shaking, I grooved it out, serenading her.

"Where is your poop?

Oooohhh

I want your poop

Aaaahhhhh

Show me your poop, give me your poop, I want your poop

Oooohhh

I want your poop

Aaaahhhhh

Give me your poop

Oooohhh

Where is your poop?

Poop poop poop.

Poop poop poop."

She kicked out a few times, and I took that as a sign of appreciation. That song was a keeper, and we both knew it. I moved into some accent work. "Ve have vays of making you poop," I said, in villain German, before swerving about five thousand kilometres. "In Ruuuuuussia, nappy changes zou."

Her hands balled, perhaps at the admittedly lazy stereotyping. Once her new nappy was on, I hoisted her back up, careful to support her little head. She farted and then, a sound like someone jumping up and down on a carrier bag full of playdough: a kind of tearing squelch. I knew that sound well by this point. It could be only one thing. It could be only poop.

"Aaaah," I said, jubilant. "You want an encore? Sure thing, baby. I need these changes more than you."

I gently put her back down on the changing mat. "Looking good, kid. Looking fresh, looking sharp."

I know I said this book wouldn't be about hacks, guides, checklists, and things you can learn on YouTube, but this is the one exception: nappy changes.

Why? Because it matters. Mama has the breastfeeding market cornered. You offer household chores, nappy changes, some cuddles, and… that's about it, at the moment. You need to show the kid you're special too. Want them looking forward to this one-on-one baby-papa time. And there's going to be a lot of it, too. Up to twelve changes a day during the fourth trimester.

Hopefully, before the baby was born, you put in quite a few hours of prep at the Nappy Changing Station (NCS)—tiny pencil behind your ear, paper blueprints unrolled across the elephant-themed changing mat—measuring, tweaking, testing, training. The daddy books usually recommend practising changes on a teddy bear, which is a good stand-in for a sleeping newborn, maybe. If you want to understand what it's like to change a two-year-old's nappy, practice on a cat (feral).

The earliest changes are the most difficult because, at first, newborns poop a tar-like substance called meconium. It's everything they swallowed in the womb: amniotic fluid, skin cells, mucus, and even their own hair. *Yum.* It's quite hard to remove, especially because a newborn's skin is thin and sensitive, so vigorous rubbing is out. Cotton wool wet with lukewarm water combined with a firm dab works well.

Here's a guide to the perfect nappy change:

1: Sex plays a role

By the fifth or sixth change, even the most inattentive father should have an inkling of their baby's sex. *Good, Papa.*

If your baby is XX, you can expect a small amount of blood in the first day or two after birth. It will look disconcertingly like a first period. This is from hormones passed on by her mother. It's nothing to worry about. What you should worry about is ensuring that you're only ever cleaning top down, vulva to butt, never the other way, which could introduce bacteria into the vagina.

XY babies come with their own hose, and you can expect to be sprayed often. There's something about the fresh air that sets them off. They sell little shields called pee guards, pee-pee teepees, and others with even more awful names. You can also just take a muslin cloth, fold it, and place it over the penis. You have a lot of muslin clothes, right? They're magical.

2: Keep one hand on the baby at all times

While changing your little one, always keep one hand on them. Common reasons to visit the ER include accidental burns from hot mugs of tea and injury from babies' wriggling off the changing table. They're slipperier than a Vaseline snake.

3: Put on a show

Just because your audience is captive doesn't mean you can't entertain them. Razzle *and* dazzle. The NCS is a great place to tease out the sharper edges of that new stand-up comedy routine.

4: Make the change

All the guides and books and courses emphasise how gentle you need to be during the change. I see scant evidence for this. Babies are tough little buggers. You should be as gentle as possible, of course, but you also don't need to handle them as if they're a priceless Fabergé egg you're holding for a ruthless jewel thief.

When changing a wet nappy, open then wait a few seconds before sliding it out. That way, if they pee, you have something to catch it in. For a crappy nappy, lift their feet up nice and high, otherwise they'll kick and get poop on their legs and feet. Breastfeeding poops are very liquid and will often run out. It's one of the reasons babies wear rompers—they help hold the nappy in place.

Once they can roll over, distraction is imperative. Give them something to hold. Or, even better, give them seven things. Drown them in sudden object showers to keep them still.

5: Don't be rash about rashes

If your nether regions spent as much time taped up as theirs do, you'd be sore too. You can expect nappy rashes. In advance, buy the creams you'll need to alleviate them. No one uses talcum powder anymore because it's rubbish. Zinc is magic. Try to give them at least fifteen minutes a day nappy free, just to air everything out. After a bath is a great time.

6: Celebrate

Once it's over, thank them for their co-operation. A high five, however limp from their side, can be enjoyable. Say "Good job, team." Because you're a team, even if they're only contributing cuteness at this early stage.

7: Stay organised

Each evening, after the little cherub is asleep, make it a ritual to survey your NCS. Perform a quick stock check, tidy, and replenish. Thank it for its work.

I Love You

You're in the baby's room and have just completed a flawless nappy change. You weren't grabby at all. You were smooth. Your grip firm, yet fair. It's the end of your second day as a father. He's now lying on a muslin cloth that's fresh, clean, just washed the previous day—one of the many services you provide your spawn that he's neither aware of nor grateful for. He wriggles as if burrowing upwards. You stare down at his big brown eyes and silly, inscrutable face, and you feel… a hot flush of love.

The first. *Hurrah.*

There have been emotional flushes in this first week, of course. You've been tearing up often—even when emptying the bins yesterday, what was that all about?—but in this wave of emotion, love is there, the feeling familiar, ancient, and sturdy.

A great relief, too, for it feels as if Mum's fallen faster for him than you; she's so smitten.

"I love you," you say, stroking your baby's belly softly with one finger. Your father didn't say it enough, and you'll right that wrong. "Whatever you need, I will do. Within reason. I will love you more than I do in this moment, many hundreds of times more, but know I love you still."

He makes a gurgling sound that reminds you of an asthmatic frog. His little head tips to the side as his eyes meet yours, briefly, before lolling away like shy marbles. He pukes a trail of half-digested milk that splashes on the nice, clean, crisp muslin cloth.

You place a hand under his head and neck and gently lift before pulling the soiled cloth away.

"Magic," you say, as you pull another one off the pile and slide it under him.

Burping

"Runa, drink or get off," Evelyn said, lying on her side on the couch, birth pillow under and around her. "Don't you dare fall asleep on them again."

It was our third day at home. Runa was just finishing a feed, or at least a snack. She'd certainly hung out there for a long time, and I couldn't blame her.

"Hand her here," I said, tired of hearing Evelyn's moaning about the sorry state of her on-fire nipples.

"I thought she and I might cuddle," Evelyn said, interrupting the German nursery rhyme she was singing. "She'll be asleep in a minute, anyway."

"Only if I burp her."

Evelyn's eyes narrowed. "Why do you keep doing that?" she asked, with her usual tone of authority. "You don't need to burp babies."

"Quick," I said, flapping my hand, gesturing for her to give Runa over before she got so full of gas that she popped like a birthday balloon in the mouth of a puppy.

"Babies are self-burping," Evelyn said.

"This a German thing?" I asked. "All British people burp their babies."

"No, hunny, it's a common-sense thing. Does anyone burp you?"

"No."

Her head kinked. "Well... so?"

"But she's a baby."

"Do you think the power to burp comes with puberty? That all babies suffocated en masse in a big gassy pile before someone worked out that you need to burp them?"

"Err," I said, moving over to the empty chair. "I suppose... yes?"

Evelyn stared down at Runa, whose tiny tongue was sticking out, as usual. "If I thought she could understand how much you're embarrassing yourself, I'd cover her ears."

"I'm going to have to sit down," I said, even though I'd already sat down. "My mind is a bit blown." I looked around the room, taking a moment to admire its many mystery plants, all of which I kept alive with tremendous ease. Evelyn had no green to her fingers, had murdered every bit of horticulture in her home before I'd moved in and taken over. Since then, everything had flourished; the place was an almost-jungle.

"Actually, can you take her?" Evelyn asked. "I'd like a break and maybe even a poo."

I wafted my hand. I was busy. "But it's in all the movies and TV shows?" I said, still hung up on the whole burping thing.

"Yeah," Evelyn said. "Everyone's water breaks at the start of labour and women give birth in under a minute too."

"I'm pretty sure my parents burped me."

"You *can* burp a baby, obviously. It's not, like, illegal or something. It's just unnecessary."

"They lied to me," I said.

Evelyn slapped her forehead.

"Don't slap your forehead. I don't want Runa watching that and then slapping her forehead at me every five minutes like you do."

"She's a baby. She doesn't even know she has hands."

"Now, yeah."

"Well, be less ridiculous, then?"

"They lied to me," I said, again. "All of them."

As we discussed in *Dad Differently: Pregnancy and Birth*, popular culture is an untrustworthy guide to follow through the maze of parenting. It contains many stupid ideas, revealed in movies and TV shows and watched by parents-to-be, who repeat them.

Why does this matter? Well, *Mr Noboobs*, with your task list full, you need ways to save time and lower the family's stress levels. Here are some tasks, concerns, and responsibilities you can probably ignore during the first year.

1. Burping them

I've looked into it, and Evelyn was right, mostly. Some parents (often those with colicky children) swear it helps, but the belief that you need to burp your baby after a feed doesn't hold up under scientific scrutiny. It's a thing you can do, sure, and a thing you might even like doing, but it's not a thing your child *needs*. Because babies are self-burping.

2. Heating the milk

If you're bottle-feeding or supplementing, most babies don't care what temperature the milk is, just that they get it when they want it. They care about that a lot, and they'll let you know loudly if you're dawdling.

3. Being quiet

The trope of everyone creeping around their house while the baby sleeps is pure, unadulterated balderdash. Once they're in a deep sleep (usually after about fifteen minutes), you could put them next to the main stage at a death-metal concert and they wouldn't wake up. My theory, backed by absolutely nothing at all, is that since they can't defend themselves anyway, there's just no advantage to being a light sleeper.

4. Bathing them every day

The parenting days are long and often kind of uneventful, so, yeah, you can bathe a baby every day if you want (sponge baths are recommended until the umbilical-cord stump falls off). It's often quite delightful to do so, but they don't *need* it. Instead, you can just take a wet cloth and use it to keep their face, neck, hands, and genitals clean.

5. Buying toys

Anything is an infant's toy. ANYTHING. There is little that gives a six-month-old more joy than a spatula, or a one-year-old more delight than an empty cardboard box. You don't need toys, you just need things, and your home is already full of things.

6. Worrying about spoiling them

You cannot spoil a baby. They live entirely in the present.

They have no concept of the before, or after. Neither cause nor effect. So, no matter what Grandma says, you can't give them too much attention or pick them up too often (if they're into that). Babies cannot be mollycoddled. Shower them in your love.

7. Deciding who they will become

As the first year progresses, you may be shocked to see with how much of a distinct, consistent personality your baby has entered the world. We parents love to believe we have influence over how our children turn out, and we do—in the genetics we (and the partner we picked) contributed. The biggest part of loving your kid is accepting who they already are. For much more on this, I recommend the book *Selfish Reasons to Have More Children*, by Bryan Caplan, who writes, "Accept that your children's lives are shaped mostly by their genes and their own choices, not by the sacrifices you make in hopes of turning them into successful adults."

Nurture does play a role, sure, but it's greatly exaggerated. And that role, however much smaller than 50 percent it might be, is spread between you and everyone else they'll interact with—siblings, family, neighbours, teachers, friends, peers. "The idea that parenting has become the overwhelmingly most important gauge of how a child will turn out is completely implausible," says Dr Ellie Lee.

8. You can't apply what you're learning to other babies

I know it's nice to think that by having a baby, you learn how babies work. That you're picking up transferable parenting skills. You will grow in confidence, that's true—so much so that you'll decide to pick up a friend's baby and plonk her on your hip, just the way your baby loves, only to watch her explode with anger. Every baby is unique. Some love to be carried face out. Others need to see their parents at all times. Some love to be cuddled and swaddled. Others like being left the hell alone. It's really disappointing how nontransferable it all is—not only between your baby and all others, but between your baby and another of your babies, should you have more.

As Evelyn says, "Thinking 'I have a baby, I know babies' is like saying 'I have a girlfriend, I know women.'"

Show You're Scared Too

The weeks passed, Evelyn healed, the midwife visited several times, and other than niggles with breastfeeding, Runa was doing well. We were learning about her temperament—about how she craved body contact at all times. How she adored the koala grip. How, unlike many of our friends' babies, she didn't need to be rocked to sleep or jiggled while awake.

We were barely learner parents anymore. It was time to leave the house. I was excited to show Runa off to the world.

On the way to a nearby park, her in the koala grip on my forearm, I was sure everyone was admiring her. She was so tiny. And so wonky. We lay down in the park, basking in the fresh air and sun. In that moment, only a fool would have denied we had everything, all of it, every drip, drop, and dram of the world's blessings.

"I think I get it now," Evelyn said. "Why when they do those studies and ask parents if they're happier than before they had kids, they say yes, but then when they, like, drill down and measure, they're actually less happy." She looked down at herself. "I'm full of anxiety, I'm fat, sleep deprived, my vagina's a crime scene, I can't listen to music without weeping, my breasts are leaking, but I feel so goddamn happy. There's just so much love in my life right now." She then shrieked loudly.

I leaped up, assuming that Runa, asleep between us on the blanket, must have caught on fire. I saw no fire. "What?"

"Ant," she said, pointing furiously. "There's an ant near her leg. Get it. *Quick*."

I sat back down.

"What are you doing?"

"Sitting back down."

"Don't sit down—get the ant!"

I sighed. "It's an ant."

"KILL IT."

"What's an ant going to do to her?"

"I WANT IT DEAD. I'M NOT HAVING ANTS ON MY BABY."

"Okay, okay." I reached down over Runa and splatted the ant. "I've killed the ant now, but I mean, really. *Jesus*."

Evelyn burst into tears, which was the last thing I needed. "What now?" I asked.

"Poor ant," she said, between sobs.

"You wanted it dead."

"I overreacted. I'm sorry."

"Apologise to the ant, not me."

"It might have had *children*," she said, her voice cracking.

"I don't think that's how ants work."

"Well," she said. "It had a mother, didn't it?"

"Sort of."

I handed her a tissue from the baby bag. We had tissues everywhere. Our life was one big tissue. She blew her nose. "I feel like that ant that's controlled by the parasite," she said. "Do you know what I mean?"

"Why are you still talking about ants?"

"You know what I mean, though, right?" Her eyes pleaded. She really needed me to know about the ant. To be where she was: *looney land*. "The ant that gets its brain hijacked, I mean? I feel like that. Like motherhood has possessed me and I've become this crazy mess and I'm just desperate to martyr myself for her. To show how much I care, to prove to myself I can be a mother, you know?"

"No," I said, wrinkling my nose.

She hit me on the arm. "You being calm and rational and making fun of me doesn't help, okay? It doesn't fucking help."

"Okay," I said.

"Why are you not freaking out?" she asked.

"I'm freaking out. I freak out all the time. I checked she was breathing four times last night."

"You don't look like you're freaking out."

"We're in a park," I said. "We have all the world's blessings. And anyway, you got all the good drugs. I'm mostly just me, but with a baby, who is actually quite chill most of the time."

She crossed her arms. "I'm scared."

I slid around Runa to cuddle her mother, who nuzzled in against my chest. "Me too," I said. "All the time."

"You have to show me how you're scared too, okay? I can't just be alone with it."

"Okay," I said. "I'll try. But you're also two weeks into a new job that you can't quit for twenty years, that has twenty-four-hour-long shifts, and that's unpaid. Oh, and if you do it badly, someone dies. Give yourself a break already."

"I'll try," she said, but then screwed her eyes really tightly closed.

"What?"

"There's another ant."

"Do you want to go home?" I asked, knowing something had happened to the woman I loved but not having a word for it yet.

"Yes," she said. "Help me up."

Micromumming

It was my friend David who coined the verb that finally explained what had happened to Evelyn. It happens to many new mums. Deprived of sleep and pumped full of both natural hormones and artificial painkillers, they can become erratic and muddled, briefly unable to sort the parenting pertinent from its irrelevant—i.e. ants.

"Can I come hide at yours for a few hours?" David asked me one day over the phone.

"Why? What's going on?"

"Petra's *micromumming* hard over here about socks. I need a break."

I laughed. "Sure."

Micromumming is likely to happen throughout the fourth trimester. Think of it as excess maternal concern directed at imagined threats and irrelevant parenting minutia. It's often accompanied by phrases such as "I know it probably doesn't matter but..."; "Just to be on the safe side I'm going to..."; and, "Is this mark on his leg new? Oh god, what do we do? CALL AN AMBULANCE."

When taking his infant son out, my friend Nick, so used

to his partner's micromumming, would close the apartment door and then immediately, right there in the hallway, remove a superfluous layer of clothing from his son. He'd leave it there by the door then put it back on again before he walked inside.

It's not your partner's fault, of course—it's the enormity of the job. Everyone expects her to be naturally good at this, while they expect very little of you. Oh, and it's also the hormones.

Oestrogen and progesterone, which can rise to 100 times their normal levels during pregnancy, are dropping hard. Oestrogen dips by 90 percent within the first twenty-four hours of birth[1] and progesterone to pre-pregnancy levels within five days[2].

Cortisol, usually two to four times its normal levels during pregnancy[3], remains elevated for several days after birth.

Oxytocin, high because of breastfeeding, can make that bond feel so intense and precious, it's natural that any threat to that seems grave[4].

Prolactin, responsible for the production of breast milk, is also a likely cause if breast feeding. It's at roughly twenty times its normal level and has been linked with sleepiness[5] and emotional swings[6].

It will all settle down, in time.

Normal

Our midwife, Marina, was at our place. I decided to delicately raise a concern I had. "So," I said, with feigned nonchalance. "Runa poops like five times a day. Is she broken?"

Marina laughed. "No, that's normal."

"Five times a day is normal?"

"Yep."

"But our friends' baby only poops every second day?"

She nodded. "Also normal. Eight times a day to every eight days is the normal range."

This time, I laughed. "That's a very, very wide range."

"Yes," she said. "Everything with babies is like that. Parents worry unnecessarily because they've no idea how wide a range 'normal' is."

Once the novelty of having a baby starts to wear off, your mind might drift from the current normal into the future. You'll love who they are, sure, but you'll also start fantasising about how much deeper the relationship will become once you can throw a ball together in the garden, play dominoes on the living room rug, or tease apart the contradictions in nihilism over spag bol (which they've cooked for you).

But while you're gazing longingly at future milestones, you're not enjoying where you are. The moment, they call it, I've heard. You'll grow impatient and compare your baby to other babies. If their rivals (and you do see them as rivals) reach key milestones first—walking, talking, sleeping through—you'll conclude your kid is, well, a duffer.

They're not. It's normal because, as Marina said, when it comes to babies and children, normal has a very broad definition. Normal is roomy. Normal wears spandex. Whatever normal is at that moment, make your goal squeezing as much from it as you can. Because soon it will be gone. And it's never coming back. And as hard as it is to imagine right now, you're going to miss the hell out of it.

Though your baby is on their own clock, here's a quick guide to roughly what you can expect to see in a "normal" first year.

0–3 months:
Turns head towards light
Lifts head briefly
- Probably during tummy time.
Responds to sounds
- But never your favourite bands.
Follows objects with eyes
- Sometimes both eyes.
Smiles socially
- But only at your enemies.
Begins to coo and babble

3–6 months:
Reaches for and grabs objects

- Knives, mostly.
Sits with support
Laughs and squeals
- Ideally at your great jokes.
Rolls over
Imitates sounds
Shows preferences for certain people and toys
- You. It'll be you. And a red truck. You don't even know
where that red truck came from. Did you find it somewhere?
Why are two of its wheels missing? Why won't the baby take
it out of her mouth? The appeal of this red truck will always
be lost on you until, in a fit of jealousy, after one and a half
beers, you'll throw the red truck away. Yes, you are that
petty.

6–9 months:
Stands with support
- Next up, dancing.
Crawls, scoots, or pulls to stand
- My god, she's mobile—let the babyproofing begin.
Says first words, likely *mama* and *dada*
- Although you're sure it's going to be *dada*, and you'll put in
the hours to make it so, statistically speaking, it's more likely
to be some derivative of *banana*, like *nana*, or some other
random word for something that's never changed even a
single one of the dope's nappies.
Plays peekaboo
Begins to show stranger anxiety
- This will come and go in quite distinct phases from here
on, for the first two years, but only at really inopportune
moments.

9–12 months:
Points to objects or people

Responds to simple commands

- The most common response being to ignore them.

Begins making simple gestures, such as waving and clapping

Uses *mama* and *dada* correctly

- A short phase because they soon discover how hilarious it is to use *mama* and *dada* incorrectly.

Walks with support or independently

- It's completely normal if this happens any time from eight months to eighteen months. This is the milestone about which parents are the most competitive, for some strange reason. Because once they can totter, life gets worse rather than better, as the time-to-possible-deadly-hazard shrinks enormously. And once they can walk, they'll soon be able to run…

Baby Blackjack

Thank god the crying has stopped, you think; that was a hard few hours. You look down at your phone. Somehow, entirely against your will, it has become 3am. The baby is calm now, at last, asleep at a weird angle in the nook between your bicep and chest. You're tracing an L around the living room, at a speed halfway between walking and running—a fast stride, more or less. The baby loves your fast stride.

How many laps of the living room have you completed already? Ten? Fifty? One hundred and fifty? Have you ever been this tired?

No, you answer, resoundingly. Never. Not even close. On lap one hundred and fifty, you eye the sofa lovingly.

Could you stop, you wonder? Could you sit down without waking your jailer?

You don't know. It would be a gamble. You used to like to gamble, and why not? There's nothing quite like the casino, is there? The smell of the felt, the sparkle of the lights, the spike of adrenaline as you shove your bright plastic chips around. You knew the game was rigged, but you also knew, in the short term, miracles could happen.

You don't go to the casino anymore. Where would you find the time? How could you justify that sort of financial frippery? In fact, someone looking at your life from afar might think you're no longer one of life's high rollers.

They're wrong, of course. You gamble. You gamble all the goddamn time. And the stakes have never been higher.

As a new parent, all day long you're playing hands of high-stakes Baby Blackjack: Can you reach that extra cushion over there and slip it behind your back without waking him up? Can you put him down without jolting him from sleep so you can run to the bathroom before you pee yourself, which you're going to do imminently? Is he in deep-enough sleep that you can stand up and creep out of his room without your left knee clicking loudly, as per usual, and jolting him awake?

Stupid loud left knee.

And now, at 3am, in the living room, fast striding, you're playing it again. You look down at the hand you've been dealt this time; it's not great, but it is, at least, asleep.

If you twist and manage to pull off such a bold transloca-tion as sitting on the sofa without waking Bébé up, you could rest your weary eyes and legs. You wouldn't need to carry his weight any more. Undoubtedly, you would be much, much more comfortable. You might even sleep.

But if you lose the bet, and sitting wakes him up, then... well... *bust.*

He'll be awake. Loud. Angry.

That will wake your partner.

She'll be awake. Loud. Angry.

You'll have to calm her too, somehow. And so, *Stick or twist, Papa?*

Baby Whisperers

Runa and I were in the park with a new friend from our birthing course. Runa started to cry. I picked her up and rocked her. "Oh no," new friend, Simone, said. Her daughter, Marlene, was sleeping on the other side of the picnic blanket.

"It's fine," I said.

"But she's crying."

"Yep."

"What's wrong, do you think?"

I shrugged.

"Bellyache?" she suggested.

I shrugged again.

"Tired, maybe?"

"Maybe," I agreed. "She had a bad morning, too."

"Hungry? Yes, I think it's hunger. She also had the sun in her eyes."

I stopped rocking her and looked down. We were in the shade. We were very much in the shade. "When?" I asked.

"Maybe twenty minutes ago?"

I lost the ability to blink. "She just cries sometimes," I said. "Probably having a bad day."

After a few minutes, Runa stopped crying and fell back to sleep. I put her down on the blanket, still very much in the shade.

Five minutes later, Marlene started mewling. "Shh, shh," Simone said, picking her up. "It was just a wasp."

"What wasp?" I asked, looking around.

"It was half an hour ago," Simone said. "But they're on a delay. So…"

"It stung her?"

"No, it just buzzed near her."

Marlene cried louder and louder and was rocked harder and harder. "Her hat fell off earlier too," Simone said. She looked around. "And two blankets over are playing the Who. She hates the Who."

I laughed and relaxed.

"Why are you laughing?"

"No reason," I said, knowing that this friendship was doomed.

Runa started crying again.

And again.

And again.

And then just didn't really stop, no matter what I tried. "I think I'll take her home," I said, eventually.

There will be many days when your baby will be a bit off. You'll try all your tricks—winding, rocking, jiggling, cuddling, feeding, putting on the twinkling lights they like, singing "Frère Jacques" (their favourite song)—but nothing will help. They'll scream, yell, cry, and then sob, and it will tear at your heartstrings. It'll be hard not to take it personally. You'll feel as if you're failing at your job. You'll want there to be something you can do.

What the hell is wrong with them?

You expect there to be an answer, don't you? Even though you don't always have one for when you feel like this. When you're having one of those days. And anyway, why shouldn't they be grumpy? They can't do anything and live in a land of giants. They close their eyes in the living room and open them in a park. Someone shoves a nipple in their mouth. Now a terrifying noise is growing louder and LOUDER. You know it's just a lawnmower, but they don't know about lawns and their need for cuts.

Now their bottom is wet. *Great.* They decide they want that object over there, the can of Coke. They can't reach it though, can they? Everything they want is out of their reach because they don't know they have arms. Now they're being jiggled again. It's maddening, it is. OH NO, another incoming nipple, even though they're not hungry, only spat out a nipple five minutes ago. And why is there only ever one thing to eat/drink in this goddamn world?

They close their eyes, briefly open them, and now they're somewhere else entirely. Back at home. And on their front, too. Who put them on their front? Doesn't everyone know by now how much they hate being on their stupid, useless belly? To whom can they complain about this oppressive tummy-time regime?

It's a lot. And they've had enough. And they just want it to stop. But it doesn't stop. Won't ever stop. And so, they cry a lot. And it's killing you, that noise, that pain. You've tried everything, twice.

Relax, Papa.

Absolve yourself.

You're never going to know what the problem is. Sure, you can become a Baby Whisperer, like Simone. You can decide that every one of your baby's outputs has an explain-able input. It might even calm you, that belief, but no matter how confident you sound when you say that your six-week-old baby hates the Who, it won't be true.

It's just one of those days. Their suffering will end. It always ends. Until then, remember—just as when you're sitting in bumper-to-bumper traffic, late for work, you're not stuck in traffic, you *are* the traffic—they're not giving you a hard time; they're having a hard time.

Hug them.

Bear witness.

Co-suffer.

Wait.

The Breastapo

By now, you know that having a baby is great—the joking around, the cuddles; seeing their personalities blossom; enjoying all those lovely, vicarious firsts.

You also know that having a baby is kind of, well, sort of... tedious, isn't it? The first hour of each day is magical, sure, but no one really needs that tenth hour, do they?

If you could get out of that tenth hour, you probably would, wouldn't you? And don't even get me started on the gruelling eleventh, twelfth, thirteenth, fourteenth, and fifteenth hours.

I don't think we're the first men to feel this way, either. In fact, I believe that long ago, a secret cabal of us got together and tried to figure out a clever hack to offload all the shitty, tedious, painful, sleep-destroying, back-breaking tasks in the first year of parenting to our women.

It wasn't easy.

These dads brainstormed long into the night. Filled up flip chart after flip chart. Ate cookie after cookie. Drank coffee after coffee. Covered the room and themselves (hilarious!) in sticky notes.

It didn't look promising until... a hand at the back went up. Everyone turned. "Women have breasts, right?" a timid voice asked. There were some nods and murmurs. The voice grew louder. "But we don't have breasts, right?" More nods. Louder murmurs. One man felt his chest, just to be sure. "So, if we can convince women of the importance of breastfeeding, most of the early work of parenting would be theirs, right?"

Stunned silence became loud and enthusiastic clapping. They threw their heads back and howled up at the moon. Maybe. One walked up to the flip chart, turned the page, and, with great ceremony, wrote *BREAST IS BEST*.

This shadowy cabal became known as the Breastapo. For more than half a decade, they've worked tirelessly to reduce men's first-year parenting workload by spreading a few key lies.

1. Breastfeeding is "natural"
Because everyone loves natural things, except, like, plagues and tsunamis and Parkinson's disease.

2. Breastfeeding is convenient
And it is—for the baby, who will wake up your partner three times a night, at his convenience, to suck really slowly on her breasts for hours, until they bleed.

3. Breastfeeding has enormous health benefits
Except that formula has been great for decades and so there are no longer any *meaningful* health benefits to breast milk (if you have access to clean water and reputable formula—the whole developed world, basically).
I didn't say no benefits; I said no *meaningful* benefits. If you want to read more about the scientific data on breastfeeding and all the other major parenting decisions you'll have to

make, I highly recommend the no-nonsense, data-driven books *Expecting Better* and *Crib Sheet*, by Emily Oster, who concluded, "There is certainly no evidence that breastfeeding is any worse for a baby than formula. And maybe there are some early-life benefits in terms of digestion and rashes, which you may or may not think are important. But what the evidence says is that the popular perception that breast milk is some kind of magical substance that will lead your child to be healthy and brilliant is simply not correct... The vast majority of the claimed benefits of nursing simply do not hold up when we look at the best data."

4. Breastfeeding is free
Which is true, if you don't value your partner's sleep, time, or equality.

In recent times, people have slowly been starting to see through the Breastapo's propaganda and, armed with mountains of cold, hard science, are learning the truth: breast is maybe, like, a teeny, tiny bit better. A rounding error better. And that's only if you look exclusively at infant health and not at Total Family Happiness (more on that later).

That said, the Breastapo still exert a lot of societal pressure, having many doctors and woo-woo-leaning midwives on their ideological payroll. As a father, it's important (even though their lies benefit you) to neither believe the Breastapo, nor let your partner tie her identity as a mother to breastfeeding.

Breastfeeding in the first days or weeks makes sense. The pre-milk, colostrum, really is nutrient rich. And by breastfeeding for a week or two, your partner can see how well she and the baby take to it. Your partner can determine if it helps with bonding, how much milk she has, and how convenient it is for the family as a whole.

Does it make sense to continue after those few weeks?

That shouldn't be an automatic yes, as the Breastapo would have it. First, consider these questions: How well is it working? How much milk is there? How much time is it taking? Does your partner enjoy or, at least, not detest it? How soon does she want to return to work? How often is your child waking up to feed and thus interrupting everyone's (but mostly your partner's) sleep?

Don't just blindly accept the lies of the Breastapo: breast might be best for your family, but breast is not *always* best.

The Breastapo, Part 2

A man with a firm opinion on breastfeeding? How dare he rail against decades of parenting orthodoxy? He is Mr Noboobs. He cannot know of what he talks.

But I should be strongly in favour of breastfeeding, right? I'm the one who profits most from it (and I'm including Runa in that analysis). And yet, I'm sceptical of the whole endeavour.

Why?

Because of the things I've seen. All the misery of the first months of Runa's life was breastfeeding related. Evelyn really wanted it to work, even though we'd read all the science and knew that the benefits were tiny.

Infinitesimal.

A bit less diarrhoea, and better skin, perhaps. Yet, the Breastapo had their hooks into Evelyn, and so she was adamant she'd breastfeed for the first six months; maybe more.

So, she breastfed, sort of. Only Runa wouldn't latch properly. And then when she did, she didn't feed well. There was never enough milk. Runa would cry because she was hungry.

And then Evelyn would cry, too. Then she'd try again with the other breast. Same story. Runa would feed, kind of a bit, but she was always underweight, and kind of sickly looking. We both cried about this.

The midwife tried to help. Nothing helped. Neither Runa nor Evelyn could sleep properly. Eventually, Runa was breastfeeding for forty minutes of every two hours, and even that wasn't enough. We had no choice but to supplement. Our midwife taught me how to tape a thin feeding tube to my finger and put it into Runa's mouth. She would latch onto it and I'd syringe milk in there, which she loved, because she got so much, so fast, for such little effort. She'd bawl her little eyes out when the milk stopped flowing and had to go back to the leaky, inefficient, insufficient breasts.

How she hated those breasts. Evelyn grew to hate them, too.

We asked some experts. Evelyn changed her diet about six times. Nothing helped. "What are we doing this for?" I asked, after another failed round on the boobs, about a month in.

"I need to try for a bit longer," she said, in a sad voice. "Maybe it will get better."

It never got better. As Runa got bigger, we had to give her more with the syringe. She loved the syringe so much. The syringe became the bottle. She loved that even more.

We weren't the only ones having this experience. A couple from our birthing course had a similarly difficult time with the boob. The damn baby wouldn't latch. There wasn't enough milk. While our midwife was a no-nonsense, down-to-earth, wonderful punk lady, they had an esoterically minded, chamomile, Earth-Mother, Breastapo midwife. "Such a shame you can't breastfeed," she said, every five minutes of her visits. So, they kept trying to breastfeed. They didn't supplement. Their midwife said it would only turn the baby off the nipple, the so-called "nipple confusion", for which Emily Oster couldn't find reliable evidence either.[1] Anyway, their baby didn't gain weight. Mother didn't sleep. Father had to go back to work. (Interesting side note: When he told his boss he wanted to take six months' paternity leave, he was given a big pay rise to take only a month. His partner, now earning less than he was, stayed home.) Their baby ended up in hospital. The nurses told her to breastfeed for forty-five minutes of every hour, then switch to the other breast, only stopping when the baby slept.

"When can I sleep?" she asked.

"When the baby sleeps."

"But the baby sleeps on me."

They had no answer to that because they were agents of the Breastapo. The answer was obvious. The answer was staring them in the face. The answer was the tin of formula on the shelf.

"Such a shame breastfeeding doesn't work," the midwife said, when they were out of the hospital and had abandoned breastfeeding and opened the tin. They now had a baby rapidly gaining weight.

"No, it's not," they said, then told the midwife they no longer required her services. That baby is enormous now. It bullies children three years older on the playground.

Evelyn kept trying into month two, then three, hating the task more and more.

"Can we stop now?" I'd ask, every few days, seeing how destroyed she was by the stress of it.

"A bit longer," she'd say.

"Yeah, but why?" I'd ask, though I knew the answer—the Breastapo's indoctrination. Evelyn believed good mothers breastfed. And she wanted to be an exemplary mother.

Many of my male friends have similar stories. Their women pushed through and, eventually, it worked, but at great cost. I told them I was pushing Evelyn in the opposite direction, to give it up.

"But breast milk is the greatest," said my friend Mark, over a beer. "It's packed full of the finest Mother Nature herself has to offer."

"That's not true," I said. "It's like 1 percent better than formula. And 1000 percent more work."

"Yeah, but doesn't your baby deserve the best?"

"The best parents are happy, well-rested parents, no?"

"It's not about you," he said, incorrectly.

It was about us. All of us. It was about Total Family Happiness.

In the end, Runa decided for Evelyn. She became less and less willing to put in the nipple work. Somewhere around the middle of month three, it was clear Runa was out. Which was great, as it took away the decision from Evelyn, if not the guilt.

Looking back, I wish that I'd been stronger in demanding we stop sooner. It just hadn't seemed like my place. And that's why I'm pulling no punches with you. I could have reduced the suffering that two-thirds of my family endured for months, and I didn't do it—all because of the Breastapo.

I don't want you to make that same mistake. Breastfeeding is different for every woman, of course. It might work spectacularly well for your family. It might not. About 40 percent of the women we know had experiences like Evelyn's, and the same guilt too. Forty percent is a lot of unnecessary misery. I'm not saying don't do it; I'm saying don't prolong the misery for her (and your baby) out of a misguided sense of guilt or shame.

With all that said, I'd be doing you a disservice not to mention some positive examples, too. Two of our friends adored breastfeeding. The act releases oxytocin, nature's MDMA, and some women seem to get extra high doses of it, or are extremely sensitive to its effects. Our friend Petra, who also had a wonderful pregnancy, was high as a freaking kite the whole first year because of breastfeeding. She was so loved up that when her partner, David, would take the baby out for more than an hour, she'd have to look at photos of her on her phone.

I'm not joking.

I've seen Petra on MDMA, and it's nothing compared to Petra on breastfeeding. It was the same with a friend of hers, Tabby. She adored the special bonding time with her baby. She thought it was, and I quote, "The hottest shit ever." After eighteen months, Tabby stopped breastfeeding, or rather, her baby stopped being interested in breastfeeding. What had been so very high had to come crashing down. "I felt as if I saw my baby for the first time," Tabby said. "How she really is. She's great, don't get me wrong. But she's just a baby. Like other babies. Not, like, her own genre. Not a masterpiece. I was drugged," she said, "basically. Drugged by breastfeeding."

Eventually, Petra's kid lost interest in the boob, too. It was just too much work compared to eating real food, albeit pulverised. Her daughter ended that part of their relationship almost overnight. Petra, an addict, was forced to go cold turkey. She fell into what she now describes as a "hormonal depression." It took two months for her body to adjust to piddly, normal amounts of oxytocin.

"If we have a second child, how long would you breastfeed for?" I asked Evelyn recently.

She didn't even have to think about it. "Two weeks. To see if it would go better this time. If it didn't, I'd stop and not feel even slightly guilty about it."

The Most Thing

With the first weeks over, you have your routines, your hair is less on fire, and life coalesces around a new, erratic normal.

You're not necessarily expert parents yet, but you've a feel for your baby's quirks and slowly, with your systems in place, you're reentering the world. Depending on the generosity of the social system where you live, one of you might also be returning to work, meeting old friends and colleagues. The ones with kids will nod, wink, shake your hand, welcome you to the club, and then get back to whatever they were doing. The ones without kids will linger, peppering you with questions to show they're interested or mine you for information because they're trying to decide if they want to have children one day.

The questions are all terrible:

So... how's fatherhood?

Would you recommend it?

Going to have another one, you think?

Is it the greatest thing you've ever done?

They mean well, of course. Everyone almost always

means well, but that's not really the point. The point is that they're missing the point.

Out of politeness, you mumble an answer, something like "Err, yeah, well, you know, it's hard, but it's also great."

That isn't what you're thinking, of course. What you're thinking is more like:

Something very profound has happened to me. For perhaps the first time in my life, I have done something I can't take back, quit, reverse, or divorce. My life is no longer my own. I am tethered to another human, and the wider humanity project, in an intricate, intractable way that I simply wasn't before.

The stakes have been very much raised.

That's why I can't review it for you in these normal terms, as if it's that all-inclusive safari holiday I took in Tanzania. I'm now the guardian of a human consciousness until it's ready to guard itself. In the meantime, the amount of suffering I could inflict upon it is immeasurable.

It is reasonable to believe everything I've ever felt—overwhelming, wonderful, awful, angst-ridden, cruel, confusing, trauma-inducing, therapy-demanding, and soul-shaking—my child will feel too. I know how pitch black my darkest days were. And worse, I know that all he will feel, he feels *because* of me. Because I made him exist, and entirely without his consent. I can justify that, just about, because I think existence is better than non-existence but, honestly, on those darkest of days, it's close.

I will have to watch my child learn he is mortal. That not everyone on earth wants what's best for him. That some people are simply mean, violent, abusive, sadistic, and will take more than he wants to give, by force. That his world, currently just cuddles, rattles and peek-a-boo also has slaves, racism, rape, murder, and asbestos.

Oh, and he will have to watch me and his mother die, too.

In fact, everyone he ever loves will die. Unless he stops it...
by dying first.

How is fatherhood?

Would I recommend it?

Am I going to have another one?

Is it the greatest thing I've ever done?

Honestly, you think, it's just the *most* thing I've ever done.

Parenting Intelligence

In German, an emotional person is described as *nah am Wasser gebaut*, which translates as *built close to the water*. It's a descriptive way of saying that they cry often, that they are easily flooded with tears.

You used to joke that you had only four emotions—hungry, horny, happy, and sad. Then you had a child. Now, you regularly wipe away a tear after you've finished wiping their butt. It's something about how they look. Or the vulnerability of that act, perhaps. The trust. The smallness. Their tiny toes. Their even tinier toenails.

You see them cuddling with your partner and you grow still and quiet as you try to control what becomes a choked sob. "I don't know what's the matter with me," you say. But you know. Having a child has moved you much, much closer to the water.

The water holds both good and negative emotions, particularly after several nights of awful sleep: sadness, anger, bitterness, resentment, desperation, disbelief at what your life has become—how micro, how routine, how not about you.

Often, you feel both the good and the bad at once. You're like a piano having all its keys pressed. Crowded House had four seasons in one day; as a new parent, you feel more than four conflicting sentiments in the same minute: adoring your baby, hating parenthood, battling exhaustion, brimming with purpose, and drowning in tedium. You're desperately sad, impossibly hungry, devastatingly grubby, and yet weirdly satisfied.

And these are just the emotions you can name. There are many you can't—shapeless, nameless lumps that sit like sand in your throat, tighten into knots in your chest, or zip around your mind as you try to nap on the sofa.

"The test of a first-rate intelligence is the ability to hold two opposed ideas in mind at the same time and still retain the ability to function," said F Scott Fitzgerald.[1] In that case, parenting intelligence is the ability to hold two (or more) opposing emotions at the same time and retain the ability to function.

Emotions are the soundtrack of our inner lives. What begins with them ends out in the world as the actions we take and the repercussions that follow for both ourselves and all the people we love.

The better you accept, without judgement, all the contradictions of how you feel, the better you'll be able to understand the bizarre, irrational behaviours of your partner and child. The better you'll be able to love and be loved.

All emotions are welcome. All emotions are valid.

Wave them in like old friends. The joy of this phase of life is not so much *what* you feel but the sheer enormity of it. The scale and grandeur and abundance. The ease with which you can be brought to tears.

How close you have moved to the water.

Part Two
The First Few Months
- Pro Parents

Write It Down

Evelyn and I were sitting in a Lebanese restaurant with friends, one of whom was first-trimester pregnant.

"We've got the twelve-week scan next week," she said.

I leaned back in my chair and adopted the authoritative tone of the village elder. "Now that's something I'll never forget."

Evelyn laughed. "You weren't there."

Everyone turned towards me. Time clunked and whirred. A cable snapped. "What? Yes, I was."

"No, you weren't. Well, not in the room."

I leaned forward in my chair. "I was in the doctor's office with you. I remember how underwhelmed I was, but I tried to hide it so you wouldn't think I was broken inside."

"It was the pandemic," she said. "No one else could come in with me. I put you on speaker phone."

"No..." I faded out.

She smiled, lowering her head and lifting her eyes. Who is the keeper of facts in this relationship? her expression asked. The one who knows all our where-we-were-whens?

"I was sitting outside," I said, now remembering. "On the street."

Everyone laughed. I sensed I was to be the butt of many future jokes.

"I can't believe you forget stuff like that," our pregnant friend said, stroking her belly softly.

"And you're not broken inside," Evelyn said to me. "You're so soppy over her."

Right on cue, I teared up. I picked up a napkin and wiped my eyes. "Well, yeah," I said. "Now she's out here and…" I looked over at her, sleeping peacefully in her pram, curled into a small ball and covered in a purple blanket. "I know she exists because she's the reason I've a dead arm, or I'm dead tired, or I want to die, or whatever. But during the pregnancy, I never really truly believed there was a tiny human inside of you." I looked down at the table. "And I definitely didn't feel anything for her, no matter how I acted."

"I'm not sure I did, either," Evelyn said.

"What? Really?"

"Yeah. I was faking it, too. It felt more like a really long bout of food poisoning or something."

"Oh," I said. "Are you dead inside as well?"

"Nah," she said. "I think it's like how you can't imagine death, you know? You also can't really imagine life."

"I won't forget," our friend said, still stroking her slight bump.

You will forget. You will forget it all—first scan, first roll, first sit, first step, first word. It's why new parents take so many photos and videos. And it's why you should write everything down, starting now, if you're not already.

How you feel.

What you're doing.

Every hope, fear, joy.

Even if it's just a sentence a day. Maybe it should just be a sentence a day. The most interesting thought you had. Hardest feeling to define. Funniest thing that happened. I didn't do this, which is why I've forgotten so much, including almost all the where-we-were-whens. That's a big part of why I'm writing these books, to capture what's left before it fades away.

You think you'll remember it all, but you won't. Write it down. Write it all down. You'll thank yourself later.

Total Family Happiness

Somehow, a dangerous belief has spread through popular parenting culture: That if you suffer for your child, that suffering is infused with nobility. That it's through martyrdom that we prove our love. This is particularly expected of mothers, who are no longer seen by society as people in their own right but as saintly vessels from which unconditional love should pour, like full-fat chocolate milk.

For many, that suffering begins with breastfeeding, but there are several big decisions coming, and if you were you so inclined/indoctrinated, you could always choose martyrdom. Most likely, because of how we've structured society, *her* martyrdom.

- Who will react first when the baby cries?
- Who will take the baby to medical appointments?
- How long are you going to breastfeed?
- Who gets the night shift?
- Who's going to stay home and who's going back to work?
- Dummy or no dummy?

- Sleep training or no sleep training?

When making these decisions, it's vital you consider Total Family Happiness (the aggregate happiness of all members in the household), because society and its traditions, expectations, and gender pay gap won't. Yes, you are parents now, but you still have needs, interests, desires, hobbies, friends, and a loving relationship that predate your children. And, logically, everything you do outside of parenting affects the time, energy, and enthusiasm you bring to childcare. Don't do (or let your partner do) things that make you sad because other people say they're natural, normal, or necessary.

Whatever we feel, we take out on the people around us, including our children. Sadness becomes hostility, resentment, and anger.

Sad you is the worst you—always.

This is why we need to break the martyrdom cycle. If we don't, your children, raised in the shadow of all that suffering, will be told, and will probably believe, that they too must suffer for their children, who will grow up and suffer for their children in an endless cycle that benefits...no one.

It benefits no one.

So, don't do it.

If you're not going to structure your lives around martyrdom, may I be bold enough to make a suggestion?

Structure your lives around sleep.

It's a simple thing, sleep. Barely even a thing. More of a non-thing—the great nightly ceasing. And that can make its importance easy to overlook. When you're living with a newborn, sleep, previously doled out in large, reliable chunks, is going to be crumblike. But lack of sleep drastically lowers your mental immune system. Without it, it gets hard to keep the irrational thoughts, worries, anxieties, stresses, fears, and concerns away. And there will be so many of those.

Sleep is your barrier.

Sleep is your defence.

Sleep is your most precious resource. Guard it at all costs. You know how they tell you not to operate heavy machinery when tired? You *are* heavy machinery.

For this reason, once Evelyn and I abandoned breastfeeding, there was no reason not to do a fifty-fifty parenting split. We were very privileged, as Germany has a generous social system, so Evelyn had a full year off, paid, and since I was self-employed, my work as a writer could be squeezed into the gaps. It would be a low-earning year, but we'd get by.

We introduced two shifts, 8am to 1pm and 1pm to 6pm, and followed this strict parenting schedule fastidiously. Evenings were usually family time and whoever didn't have night duties, would put Runa to bed. Runa barely saw the two of us in one room for the next six months. I think it was a shock when she discovered her mother and father actually knew each other. This split wasn't a romantic decision. Effectively, we chose to put our relationship on pause. It wasn't an easy decision, either, but it was one we made for sleep, and the sanity that sleep brings.

Neither of us regret it.

Pick Total Family Happiness.

Pick sleep.

Pacifiers

Evelyn took Runa to see friends. It was a glorious time that I celebrated with a nap. Then they came back. She handed me the child for my shift.

She was quiet.

She was calm.

Something was different, something was off.

"What is that?" I said, pointing at her mouth.

"It's a schnuller," Evelyn said, using the German word for *dummy/pacifier*.

"Since when does she have a schnuller?"

"She was crying and Petra suggested it. Well, she just sort of popped it in Runa's mouth, and you know what? It worked. She calmed immediately. Hasn't cried since."

I scratched my bald head. "I don't know how I feel about this schnuller business."

"What's the problem?" Evelyn asked.

"Look how content she is. She's never normally this content, not unless I'm doing all my voices and stuff."

Her head angled. "Yes. It's good, no?"

"It's just… I feel like I've been replaced by a small piece of plastic."

"I'm not sure it's plastic. Well, not the bit they—"

"You're missing the point."

Evelyn shrugged. "It's parenting on easy mode."

"Do we want to parent on easy mode?"

We both laughed. Of course we wanted to parent on easy mode.

While dummies aren't as divisive as breastfeeding, there's still some debate about them. Older generations are particularly anti-dummy, for whatever reason. Babies? They're usually pro. And why wouldn't they be? Their survival depends on sucking. It's a skill they've been practising since before birth, in utero, where they sucked their fingers. They'd probably still be sucking them after birth, too, if they had the coordination skills to put them in their mouths.

Some parents never offer a dummy because they find them ugly, or worry their baby will get addicted, but the science is unanimously positive: It's impossible for babies to suck too much. Sucking is an integral part of the fourth trimester, and one of the first steps toward self-reliance. The act lowers their heart rate, blood pressure, and stress levels, and reduces the risk of SIDS and suffocation during sleep.[1]

Not all babies take to them, of course, but there's more reason to offer them than not. Bottle-fed babies can have a dummy from birth. For breastfed babies, it's best to wait until nursing is going well. Nursing had never gone well in our case, so there wasn't much to lose.

There are some downsides, of course. Fear of addiction is justified. Starting is easy, quitting is hard, especially if you wait until they're older than one. You'll soon have dummies in every room of the house. You'll carry three on a carabiner attached to your trousers. When you leave the house, you'll check for your phone, wallet, keys, and dummy—that's how important they'll become.

Long-term (after age three, although most experts suggest weaning them off earlier, after their first birthday[2]), it can deform their teeth, and once they talk, they're pretty much impossible to understand with the dummy in.

"I suppose it's fine," I said to Evelyn. "The dummy."

"It's better than that," she said. "It's a miracle."

Monster

"I'm just heading out to the supermarket," I said to Evelyn, as I slipped on my shoes. It was an impossibly early hour following an even more impossibly long, sleepless night. Runa was in my arms. The diaper bag was on my back. We'd been parenting for six weeks.

"You're taking Runa?" she asked.

"Yes."

"Why would you take her there?"

I stood up. "Why would I not?"

"What's in it for her?"

My eyes narrowed. I hadn't considered what was in it for her. I scratched my chin. Nothing, I concluded. Since she mostly drank breast milk at this point and Evelyn was here, I was actually taking her away from her supermarket. But then I considered what was in it for me: Mars ice-cream bars.

"I want life to feel normal," I said. "And normal people go to the supermarket. Can I not also have needs?"

Sweet, sugary, chocolate-covered needs.

"Normal people don't go to the supermarket this early to

buy ice cream," she said, unreasonably, as it was already 7:50am.

"Yeah, but the earlier you go out, the quieter it is. And how do you know I'm buying ice cream?"

"The freezer door opened then quickly closed about five minutes ago."

"It's like living with the bloody Stasi," I said, scooping Runa up. "She'll love it there."

I carried her down the stairs, taking each step slowly, watching my feet. I didn't trust my ability to drive myself on this little sleep. Sugar would help. Sugar always helped; really briefly.

At the bottom, I gently lowered my cute little life-wrecker into her pram. I shoved her all the way to the nearest super-market, which was in the basement of a horrible shopping mall where the overhead strip lights scorched the backs of your eyes and people with substance-dependence issues (substances far worse than milk) withered in quiet corners.

We entered the supermarket. Runa burst immediately into tears before we'd even reached the on-sale kumquats.

I pushed on. I sped up. She began to scream and wail, her mouth now half the size of her head, her little tongue flapping like a windsock. Evelyn was right, as usual—Runa hated it here, and we were barely even inside. Were only passing the in-store bakery, still many aisles away from Frozen Goods: the chilly belly of the beast. I considered turning back, aborting the mission, but I'd come all this way.

I wanted normalcy.

And I wanted a Mars fucking ice-cream bar.

My stress levels rose. People were looking. People were judging. When I say people, I mean, of course, women. A crying child is invisible and inaudible to most men unless it's their child; sometimes even if it *is* their child.

But not women.

Women hear everything.

Women hear it all.

If a baby or child suffers, they suffer too. There weren't a lot of them around this early, but all who were there, hurt. They stopped putting broccoli in their carts. They stopped reading the nutritional information on tins of pumpkin soup. They turned. They stared. *What is he doing to that baby? Why is he such a crap parent? Why has he brought a newborn to the basement supermarket of a horrible shopping mall where people with substance-dependency issues wither in quiet corners?*

I panicked. I could have picked Runa up, of course, and that would probably have worked. But a month and a half into parenting her, I had data on her needs. I knew she wouldn't tolerate being put back down unless thoroughly asleep. She was cuddly. Affectionate. Never, ever wanted to be alone. It was an enormous time commitment to get her that deeply asleep. And I'd need both hands.

No, I decided. It would be easier to finish the shop, get her home, and then let her sleep on me.

I'd be quick.

I left Runa and her bulky buggy at the end of the frozen-goods aisle and rushed down it, searching for... There they were, those shiny black boxes tinged with gold. I opened the freezer and, murmuring with delight, bent down and that's when I saw her. An elderly woman approaching Runa. She had a red headscarf tied over short grey hair. Another was coming too, shuffling over from Household Goods, following ancient instincts—maternal zombies of concern, readying their best unsolicited advice. We'd started receiving it during Evelyn's pregnancy, and it hadn't stopped coming.

I grabbed two boxes of Mars ice-cream bars and carried them back to the buggy.

"In my day, they wore socks," the elderly woman shouted in my direction.

She is wearing socks, idiot.

Runa was deafeningly loud now. Reluctantly, these do-gooders parted so I could dump my wares into the basket I'd attached to the buggy's handlebars. Which was when I saw Runa wasn't wearing socks. She was wearing sock. She'd had socks on when we left the house but had lost one sock. How was she always losing her damn socks?

"Sock fairies," I said.

"Perhaps she's cold?" the elderly woman said.

"Perhaps," I said, trying to move the buggy past them and away. The other one, a vexed woman in a tracksuit holding a giant spring onion, really more of a small tree, stepped across to block me. "Or too hot?"

"She might have a temperature issue, yes," I said, as I reversed and turned, whizzing from this huddle of female concern.

"Not even wearing socks," the elderly woman repeated.

"She is wearing sock."

"Pick her up?" Vexed Tracksuit Lady suggested, to my back. "The little bear. The sweet little bear."

I pushed Runa towards the checkouts. We got in line, Runa still screaming the roof down.

"Do you want to go in front of me?" the woman in front of us asked. She was about my age and had kind eyes.

"It's fine," I said. "But thanks. Probably just a stomach ache."

"Yeah," she said, smiling sympathetically. "I just go into full panic mode when I hear them cry, you know?"

"Sure," I said.

"Dummy?" a familiar but unwelcome voice asked. I turned around slowly. Yes, it was the headscarfed demon. "Did you try a dummy?" she asked. "My little one just loved it."

They had dummies back on the Ark with the dinosaurs in the Big Bang-ing ice age sixty hundred million years ago?

"Hmm," I said.

"Is that shit?" she asked, pointing into the buggy.

Shit? Oh... I suddenly remembered that, the previous evening, glued to the couch by Runa, sleeping in the koala grip, as usual, I'd shouted at Evelyn to bring me something, anything, all of the things we had made of chocolate. All she'd been able to find, at the very back of the freezer, was a single choc ice, aka the pauper's Mars ice-cream bar. Eating it went badly, and, yeah, fine, I splattered Runa; I'm not proud of it. I'd also been too lazy to change her before leaving the house, and now her romper was generously flecked with what looked exactly like poop. I looked down at myself. I was covered in what looked exactly like poop.

"It's chocolate," I said, defensively, and loudly, because Runa was still crying so damn much.

"Pick her up," she said.

"No," I said, lifting my nose high in the air as I turned back towards the till.

"Your fly is undone," she said, which was beyond or, I suppose, beneath the point. I did up my zipper and reached surreptitiously across to my pocket to check if I had a dummy. We'd started on them only a week ago, but Runa had become instantly addicted. They were her baby crack, which, coincidentally, was probably available somewhere in this horrible shopping mall.

In my right pocket I felt the soft rubber of a... yes, I hadn't forgotten it. Of course I hadn't forgotten the dummy. It was too vital already. If I gave it to her, she would quieten immediately, but it would also mean that this interfering wise-ass would be proved correct.

It would mean she would win.

And I didn't want her to win.

I paused, considering my options, consulting my conscience, and then took my hand off the dummy. The woman in front of me, Kind Eyes, paid, having packed her fair-trade vegan goods frustratingly slowly.

"Guten tag," the cashier said, when it was my turn, but it wasn't a good day at all. She scanned my goods, which didn't take long, as I had only two of them. I got out my wallet.

"Just so you know," said Kind Eyes, who'd come back, "she's lost a sock."

I turned and blinked, very slowly, as if I knew it was the last time I'd ever blink and I really wanted to make the most of it. I said nothing with my mouth but a great deal with my face.

"Do you have a payback card?" the cashier interrupted.

"It's just," Kind Eyes said, "I know how quickly my little one freezes."

"The total is €5.98," the cashier said.

"It's September," I said.

"Just thought you'd want to know."

"You're holding up the line," the cashier barked at me. Kind Eyes smiled nervously again, turned, and fled.

Outside, back in the light, I gave Runa—now as red in the face as uncooked beetroot—her dummy. It worked instantly.

We walked. My steps were heavy. I had done her wrong, my daughter. I had let her down. Placed my ego above her needs. It was the first time I had done this. I found it concerning. Would I do it often? I swore never to tell anyone about it.

My phone rang. "How's it going?" Evelyn asked.

"Great," I lied. "She was really into it."

"Can you buy yoghurt?"

"Not really," I said.

"Why not?"

"We're home now," I lied, from two streets away.

"I'll come down and help you with the shop—"

I hung up and sighed. I had done them both wrong, my women. I had let them down. Placed my ego above their needs. I swore never to tell anyone about it.

I reached down into Runa's buggy, lifted a box of Mars ice-cream bars, tore it open, took one out, ripped off its packaging, and sank my teeth into it.

I was a monster. But a monster with chocolate.

10:21am

"I can do it, I can do it, I can do it," you chant, but you suspect, deep down, that you cannot.

It's raining so heavily that you're house-locked. Having listened to every single true-crime podcast ever, twice, you have nothing with which to distract yourself as you try desperately to kill the remaining time of your parenting shift walking your daughter around your home in a continuous, persistent, soul-defeating loop.

"Rrrrarararararrrrruhhhh," she says, as you enter the kitchen, on lap four thousand and two. Your arms ache from holding her in the precise manner she favours—one hand between her legs, the other under her chin, supporting her head, propping her forwards. She's like a broken metal detector that you sweep over places. One that never beeps but does occasionally say "Rrrrararararararrrrruhhhh."

The black circular clock above the door ticks audibly.

Tick.

A second.

Tick.

Another second.

You will the seconds to speed up. They do not speed up. "Fridge," you say, showing her all the things magnetised to the fridge. Again. "Photos. We looked at them on the last lap. They're from a wedding your mother and I went to in... *somewhere*. Sweden? Norway? One of them places with cold people and beautiful climates. No, the other way round. Anyway, it's like twelve euros for a raisin, so we're not going back." You raise her up to a different photo. "I still don't know who these people are. Probably your mother knows them." You raise her higher. "Leaflet. It's for pizza. You can get a big pizza and a Pepsi for €9.99, basically. There's terms and conditions. No one reads them." You read them. "Oh, the offer expired four years ago. I should probably put that in the bin. Maybe we'll save that for the next lap, as a treat? I told you about pizza on the last circuit. The Italians invented it. It's a high-carb Frisbee, basically."

You leave the fridge. You've chiselled thirty-four seconds out of the fridge. You know because you counted them with the clock. *Tick, tick, tick, tick.* Thirty-four seconds is a win. You're happy with thirty-four seconds.

"Fancy coffee machine," you say, sweeping her right. "Got that after you were born. Totally worth it." You consider telling her about the differences between the coffee types until you realise you don't know them. "Moving on," you say, with another second in the bag. You decide to drop the word *the* from your inner and outer monologues, for a bit of a lark.

"Mmmmmmmmmammamamammamamam," she growls.

"I couldn't agree more," you say, looking around for next thing to show her as another second is claimed, owned, destroyed. And then you see it glimmering out of corner of your eye: black, circular clock above door.

Could you do it? you wonder. Should you? You could, couldn't you? When was last time you did it? No, it's too soon, surely?

Before you can answer yourself, you go and bloody well do it, don't you? You glance at circular clock and read its time: *10:21am*.

You gasp so hard you nearly drop baby.

1

-

0

-:-

2

-

1

Twenty-one minutes after tenth hour.

"My god," you say, for had it not been 10:21am multiple laps ago? 10:21am has been both done and dusted, you're sure.

"Blehbleh," your daughter says. She's no help, as per bloody usual. You consider putting *the* back in but decide no, you like thinking and talking better without it. That actually, you're going to remove *a* as well. You want to burn it all down.

Before you had child, you thought all minutes were same length. That they had been standardised like paper trim sizes. You now know how stretchy they are. How relative. That, like tree falling in forest, not making sound unless someone there to hear it, sixty seconds of minute don't pass unless someone is there filling them.

Waving baby around kitchen is not filling. It's not filling at all.

You walk said baby to kitchen table counting ticks and hover her over fork. "Fork." *Three seconds.* You take her to toaster. "It toasts." *Three seconds.* You hover her over spoon. "Kind of same as fork, but scoopier." You lower her so she can touch spoon with hand. She knocks spoon onto floor. You consider picking up spoon, but that would involve bending. Instead, you kick spoon at door in anger.

Tick, tick, tick, tick, tick, tick, tick, tick, tick, tick. Tick, tick, tick, tick, tick. Fifteen seconds.

You do few more rounds.

Here's thing.

Touch thing.

Here's other thing.

Smell thing?

Okay, then touch thing.

THING THING THINGS.

But it just isn't possible to fill so much time with activities so exquisitely mundane. Time laughs at them. Brushes them off as if they're crumbs on its wide shoulders. Familiarity really does breed contempt, you think, looking around kitchen you know so well, counting several ticks.

Tick

Tick

Ti—

Tick stops. Everything goes blurry and then sharp. *My God.* You have reached such an acute, apex level of boredom that you have stopped time entirely. You scream. That doesn't help. Annoys baby. You quieten baby. "Shh, shh, sorry my love, we just sort of broke time little bit and I'm kind of freaking out."

You listen carefully, checking again: no ticks. There are no ticks. You stare in disbelief at this silent, still, tickless place. You're scared, sure, but also oddly fascinated. Are you first one here, you wonder? Will you live here forever now in this single endless looping non-second? At least Bill Murray had whole day to play with, you think. What can you do with single endless looping non-second?

No, it's just mistake. It's just glitch. It will fix itself. You take baby back to fridge. You take baby back to toaster. Toasts. You pick up that spoon. Scoopy. It's not much, but it is something.

And, then, before you know what you're doing, you do it again. You glance up at circular clock.

10:21am

It's battery. It has to be battery, right?

Hug Your Parents

Marta, a friend of a friend, gave birth to her first child then promptly disappeared from the face of the earth.

Messages weren't delivered.

Events went unattended.

My friend asked around, but no one knew where Marta had gone. Back to Italy, was the rumour, but no one could be sure. Six months later, she appeared again, miraculously, at a brunch, as if nothing had happened.

A lot had happened, she explained, over a mimosa. After the birth, she'd fallen into a deep, listless depression. At first, the doctors thought it was postpartum, but she felt bonded to her daughter, and what little energy she could muster, she gave gladly. She rejected the diagnosis and kept looking for an explanation.

Eventually, she found it. A year before Marta's daughter was born, Marta's mother died suddenly in an accident. Marta and her mother had always had a fractious, explosive relationship, particularly through Marta's teenage years. This was part of the reason Marta had left Italy for Berlin.

"I understand now," Marta said.

"What?" my friend asked.

"All of it," she said. "When I looked at my daughter, I finally got it. My mum's fears, her doubts, her anxieties, her neuroticism. The sacrifices she made. All the work she did I didn't appreciate because I didn't know love then like I know it now. Everything she felt for me, I now feel for my daughter. And I just wanted desperately to tell my mum how sorry I was. To tell her I forgave her. I wanted to ask for her forgiveness, too. For how I treated her."

When you became a parent, you gained not only a child, but also, perhaps a new appreciation for your parents. No matter whether you had wonderful, picture-postcard-perfect caregivers or messy, middle-of-the-road mums and dads— you now have the same job, and so you know how hard it is.

How confusing. How you can't be everything, everywhere, all the time. How many promises to yourself you've already broken about the kind of parent you're going to be. Sometimes in supermarkets.

How many days you're phoning it in. How knowing you're phoning it in makes you feel.

Hug your parents. Hug them like you'll want to be hugged one day.

First Smile

I grinned down at Runa, who was on her front, under her jungle gym. It was the end of week eight, two weeks after the time the books said smiling could start.

"Ooohhh ooohhh," I said, pulling my repertoire of funny faces. Evelyn was showering, or engaging in "Mama wellness", as she called it.

"Heyyyyyyyy, heyyyyyyyy, Runa." I picked up a nearby squeaky carrot. I squeezed its stomach and it began to play the song "Row, Row, Row Your Boat." This thing made no sense at all. I threw it at the wall.

"For dads, the day the kid smiles for the first time is day one," my friend Mark had said, back while Evelyn was pregnant. "The rest is just duty. Doesn't count."

I had taken those words personally. I was determined to get that first smile. And with it, to reach day one: end of duty, dawn of pleasure.

"Soon," I said to Runa. "You will give me that smile soon."

The doorbell went. "Midwife's here," Evelyn shouted, from the bathroom. "Is it tidy in there? I need to get dressed. Make small talk."

"Tidy enough," I said, going to answer the door. Marina entered. I made both coffee and small talk. Evelyn came through in her dressing gown. We talked and drank coffee. It was lovely, as usual. Marina reassured us that we were doing well, which was all we needed to hear. Runa never cried when Marina was over. It was as if she could tell she was in the presence of a seasoned (but non-grizzly) pro.

"Height and weight check," Marina said, and we all walked to Runa's bedroom. We had done several height and weight checks by this point. We knew the drill. Height was easy; height was a tape measure, Runa on her back. Weight check? That was a bit weird. Marina would put her in a wide, flat cloth bag, as if she were purchasing her from Babies "R" Us, then hoist the bag onto a luggage scale. "Still really impressed with this setup," Marina said, about my NCS.

"Thanks." I blushed.

"Wow, you are just gorgeous, aren't you—those eyes," Marina said, as she flattened and opened the bag, sliding Runa onto it. She tickled her lightly and bent down to her, blowing a kiss. "Let's get you in the bag."

Evelyn and I hovered, soaking up all the compliments about our flawless parenting and epic baby, delighted someone else could see what was so patently obvious to us— this kid was a goddamn firecracker; definitively her own genre.

And then... there... yes... a twitching at the edges of Runa's mouth. Those lips curled upwards, and as they did, all the world's clouds parted and a great dazzling light illuminated the planet. There was, albeit briefly, peace on earth.

"She smiling," Evelyn said, pointing. "My god, look."

I couldn't look. Had to look away. The anger. The bitterness. Marina hadn't put in the work I had put in. Hadn't wiped the butts I had wiped. Hadn't had her nights broken like I'd had my… I glanced back towards Runa. Had to. Her smile had widened.

"She's smiling," Evelyn said again. "I can't believe it."

Marina giggled nervously then lifted the bag, hiding Runa. "Five point three kilograms," she said. "Still a little underweight, but nothing to worry about. Keep supplementing with formula. You've a good sense for how much. You're doing a great job, you two."

"She smiles," I said, dumbstruck. "She smiled… at *you*."

"Did she?" Marina said, lowering the bag on the NCS. The sides of the bag dropped, revealing Runa. Marina lifted her and handed her to Evelyn. The smile was gone. The gaslighting, however, continued. "I didn't see anything," Marina said. "They only smile for their parents at first."

They say you never forget the first smile. Had I got the first smile, I would have proved them wrong. I didn't get it, however, and so this time, my frustration will mean they are right.

Talking of right, so was Mark. It's my duty to report that later that afternoon I got my smile, then two more, then many more. With them, I wouldn't say duty ended, exactly. There's always some duty in caring for a baby, but there is pleasure in duty too, no? And pleasure in knowing you're doing a good job. Before the first smile, babies communicate and guide us with their crying, but once they can smile, everyone gets a nicer, more rewarding option—positive reinforcement.

Carrot, not stick.

Red

You're on the sofa, as usual. You recently dozed there, wrapped up together, the two of you. A sweet little pair. He's two months old. You aren't sure where the time went. He makes noises now, low-pitched growls and grunts.

Today, you think, as you stroke his cheek, he looks particularly Winston Churchill–like: wrinkled but in a stately way, worthy of ovation. You wipe some slobber away with a muslin cloth. You are madly, madly in love. It's taking all you have not to smother his lumpy head with kisses.

Then, suddenly, his eyes swing to the left, towards the red-and-black throw pinned to the wall, the one you got on that holiday in Tanzania. You see them focusing. He's riveted, the little bugger. "Grrgrgrgrgrgr," he says.

"What colour comes first?" you ask your partner, who's on the other couch socialising through media.

"Red," she says.

"It's here," you say. "Red has arrived."

She throws down the phone and rushes over. "How can you tell?"

"Watch."

You both watch. Yes, it's unmistakable. He's staring at the throw as he has never stared at anything before. He's mesmerised.

"Let's do a test," your partner says, and darts to the kitchen. She returns with two cups—one red, one blue.

The red. He loves the red one.

"My god," she says. "Red has arrived."

"It must be amazing for him. Such an upgrade."

"Wait until he can see hot pink."

Things settle down. Your partner returns to the great outrage machine in her pocket. You leave his cheek alone but stroke his bald head. He's still staring at the throw, at all its rich blood-red.

You feel very full. "Do you remember loneliness?" you ask.

"Not really," she says.

"Was it a kind of emptiness? Or more of a pressing feeling?"

"More like burning, I think. Because there's desire mixed in there."

"Hmm," you say. "Could be."

"I don't know," she says. "I can't remember."

"Good, right?"

"Yes," she says. "Very much so."

"I think this might be enough for me," you say.

"Enough what?" she asks.

"All of it. *Everything*. Him. You. Us."

"Let's see," she says.

The Seat

I was getting sick of schlepping that heavy-ass buggy around. Plus, Runa slept best on me. There had to be portable travel solutions, right? Ones that would let me be free of arm?

I bought a baby carrier second-hand. And then friends gave us some. Somehow, we went from none to four in a week. I put them out on the couch, in a row.

One had an instruction book, so I started there. "I'm going to need your help to get her in position," I said to Evelyn, who was waving objects in front of Runa, making her do tummy time against her will. Right now, she was waving that damn carrot that still, unfathomably, unforgivably, played "Row, Row, Row Your (fricking) Boat."

"She only likes being carried facing out," she said.

"I know that. Of course I know that." I tapped the instruction sheet. "This carrier can do it. Says so right here."

Knowing I'd need to practice, because it *was* my first rodeo, I looked around and grabbed a nearby teddy. Another gift. I picked Teddy up as I perused the instructions again, turning the page, turning it back, frowning. I put the instructions down, picked up the carrier, and opened and closed some clips. Why were there so many clips? I turned it upside down. I turned it back around. I frowned harder.

I put on what I thought was the central harness, just above my hips. A square of fabric hung limply down. I put Teddy in and lifted the flap. I clipped. It felt weird. Upside down, maybe? I took it off. No, I'd been right the first time. I turned it. I turned myself. The harnesses came off. The harness went on. Teddy tumbled to the ground, headfirst.

"They've done it wrong," I said, scratching my beard. "I'm going to e-mail them."

"That would have been a hospital trip," Evelyn said, pointing at Teddy. "Skull fracture. Let's wait a few more months, okay?"

"Why don't you just help me?"

"She's too young," she said. "And I don't want to stress her out."

"You're stressing me out. I'm not going to stress her out. I'm stressed out. And you're making her do tummy time. She hates tummy time."

"Calm down."

"Help me then?"

"Your dyspraxic," she said.

Why was she bringing that up? It was as if she wanted me to fail.

"I need to get out," I said. "I'm going bananas in here."

"Take the buggy."

"But it's so... *ugh*," I said, picking Teddy up, brushing dust off his gaping skull wound, and starting all over again. Was I folding the front flap right? But the legs... Teddy didn't have long enough legs to wedge him in there, tight and snug. He was such a stubby bear. They must really rip into him at the Teddy Bear Picnic, I thought. I wondered if that was why he was rocking the bow tie, why he'd funned himself up so.

"I went to university," I said, as I started over for the fifth time.

"Barely," she said. "You studied business."

"Okay," I said, twirling while pulling some cords. "I think I have it. Bring her over here."

Evelyn sighed but complied. "If she cries, we take her out."

"Yeah, yeah, yeah."

Runa was lowered onto the couch, on her back. Her fists were balled, but she was happy to have escaped tummy time. "Hey, you," I said, as she poked her little tongue out. "Want to come out with Papa?" I bent forward and tried to slide the fabric under her, but it was too short, so I dropped to my knees. "Lay her on this," I said, pulling it forward. "In the middle. *No.* The other middle. Lower. Arms out."

I fastened several clips. Slowly, I lifted her up, holding her head. It was going fabulously well, until…

"Her legs don't look like they should," said Mama, the pedant, reading the instructions while nibbling her bottom lip. "You're curving up her spine. You're hunching her all up."

"She's fine."

On cue, Runa started to cry.

"You're stressing her out. Take her out."

"Give me a second." I checked the picture again. I twisted left then right. I didn't look like the picture, somehow. But Runa was supported. Well, I was holding her head. Should I have to hold her head the whole time? Her wailing grew more urgent.

Evelyn stepped closer. "Shhh, my love. We'll get you out. Get her out."

I stepped away from her fussing, micromumming mama. Soon she was screaming, and I had to admit (to myself but not Evelyn) that she was massively stressed out. And why shouldn't she be? I was radiating ineptitude, as usual.

"Are we stupid?" I asked, as I opened the clips and let

Evelyn prise her carefully out.

"Shhhh," she said. "It's okay. Daddy's a bit simple. We won't let him use the carriers. I'll use them. But not now. Some more tummy time, my love?"

"They've done it wrong," I said, again. I went to the bedroom to watch YouTube tutorials, but they just made the situation worse, as always.

I wouldn't subscribe to any channels on this cursed day.

There had to be something simpler. A truly idiotproof carrier. Not that I was an idiot. I just wanted to take my child out for a walk without all the buggy hoopla. It was a problem, but it didn't feel insurmountable.

That night, when the house was silent, I plunged Amazon's commercial depths. Got really mucky, I did. It took three hours but I found it: 3D Belly Protector & EVA Massage-Board Baby Hip seat Comfy Carrier ALL-in-ONe Pro FAST SHIPPING.

It was, more or less, just a waistband with a ledge sewn on the front. You could simply plonk baby onto it and hold her there. My hands wouldn't be free, but the rest of me would be. There was nothing to clip, tighten, or straighten. No folds. No instructions. No flaps. It was just a ledge on a waistband. It was idiotproof. Not that I was an idiot.

It arrived even more quickly than they'd said. It really was fast, the shipping. "Look at this," I said, pulling it out of its box.

"She's going to hate it."

It was on in seconds. I twirled, beaming.

"You look like an idiot," she said.

"I'm not an idiot. I've been clear about that."

"It looks like you have a massive erection."

"Just give her here," I said, ignoring the comment.

The child was handed over. I sat her down. She didn't cry. Smiled, even, she did. I leaned her forwards a bit, like she loved. There was floor and she could inspect it, her number one hobby. I held her little head and skipped off to the hallway mirror. I swirled and twirled. She smiled again. She was as enthusiastic about it as I was.

"How fun is this, kid?"

"Looks stupid," Mama said, taking a photo to send to all my friends so they could mock me in seven different group chats simultaneously.

"Who cares how it looks? Right, we're going for a walk around the block. And I'm taking nothing but this seat."

"Take the baby."

"Obviously I'm going to take the baby. *Jesus.*"

It was a great walk. It was the best of walks. She was so close to me, the baby, that we could have a conversation. Almost whispering into each other's ears, we were. Although it's fair to say I did most of the talking. She could see the world better, too, and that world could see her in her shimmering, genre-defining brilliance. I pointed at many things— blue cars, a cat, our neighbour Carol who always wore ridiculous hats.

It was a great walk. It was the best of walks.

I didn't know it yet, although I suspected it, but 3D Belly Protector & EVA Massage-Board Baby Hip seat Comfy Carrier ALL-in-ONe Pro FAST SHIPPING, or, as it would become known, "the Seat," was a definer. Immediately vital to my parenting. Parenting has epochs. These might include breastfeeding, solids, crawling, walking, playground, tricycle, bike, and university. For every family they're different. Evelyn and I had two: Before Seat (BS, aptly named) and Post Seat (PS).

I would never be without the seat again. So many memories of the first year are of her and me walking around, her on that seat. More of a throne. Any idiot could see it changed the whole game. It changed everything.

She Sits

"She's sitting," Evelyn shouted, through the wall, into the bedroom.

"No way," I said, scrambling up from the bed and darting into the living room. "It's too soon."

Runa was on the white sofa, butt down, legs bent, leaning heavily to the left but sitting. Manipulating gravity. Making it her bitch.

"Jesus," I said. "It's early, no?"

"Five months," Evelyn said, "on average, I think."

"How old is she?"

"Three and a half months."

"She's a damn prodigy. Look at you," I said, kneeling to get closer. I stroked her on her favourite spot on the cheek. She smiled. "You clever little thing."

"It's from watching you," Evelyn joked.

"I'm more of a lay…" I hesitated. "Liar? No, that sounds weird. It's the Seat. It's all her training there. When do they crawl?"

"Ages yet," she said.

"Amazing," I said.

We watched our daughter, the sitter, until Runa looked down, suddenly confused by this weird configuration of limbs. Her eyebrows scrunched. Her mouth opened and closed rapidly. Uncertainty blossomed inside of her. She looked like a cartoon character who'd just noticed they'd run off a cliff.

"She's going," Evelyn said, as she tipped further and further to the left.

"Timber," I shouted, as she splatted down, onto the side of her face.

"Waahhhhhhhh," Runa said.

Evelyn picked her up. Cuddled her. "It's okay, hunny. That happens. You're doing so great."

"Perhaps not a prodigy?" I offered.

"Being a prodigy must be rubbish," Evelyn said.

"That's true," I said. "It's a long way down from prodigy."

Runa calmed. "This is high enough," Evelyn said, squashing her back down on her bum, moving her legs into position, beginning another sit.

Novelty

You slam the door behind you and trudge out to the street. You lost at Baby Blackjack last night. Got wiped out. Something was up—a tummy bug, maybe? There was a lot of very potent gas coming out of him. His belly was hard as a rock. The longest stretch of sleep you had was what, an hour?

Every time you close your eyes to blink, they stick, like an old door. Your thoughts are lumpy. You're covered in milk and drool. Before you had a kid, you used to smell discarded clothes on the floor to decide if you could wear them. Now you wear anything whose surface is comprised of less than 20 percent stains. You're a human handkerchief. More dribble falls on you in a day than drizzle falls in a year in a Scottish coastal town.

You sit him up in the buggy. He's wearing a teddy suit that zips up and has little ears on its hood. You recently swapped over from the bassinet to the actual seat. He's thrilled with its magnificent view. He looks as if he's driving a racing car. You push him to the end of the road.

It's Sunday.

No... it's Saturday.

Is it Friday?

It's a day, of that you're sure. Your steps are slow and heavy. You zip your coat up all the way. You want to cry. You do cry, just a little. Two tears. Nothing, really. You turn right and push the buggy towards the nearest park.

"Blublublublublublub," your son says.

"Yes, hunny," you say, as you swerve to avoid dog shit and, instead, trundle over broken glass that crunches under-wheel. Two corners later, this new day in this billion-year-old, tattered world has sated him and his little head droops. He is soon asleep. Lucky bastard, you think, but you raise your head and send a silent thanks to the heavens. For when he's asleep, he cannot need anything from you.

You enter the park and sit down on a handsome wooden bench painted crimson. There are two, and on the next, sepa-rated from you by a green municipal bin, sit a beautiful young man and woman, both dressed scantily, and in black. The woman, lean, firm, sprightly, has a pink feather boa. Her corset must be restricting her breathing, but she doesn't show it. The man wears leather trousers. The top three buttons of his suede shirt are open. He is audacious. There doesn't appear to be a single hair on his nubile body. They are both immune to temperature. You realise, with deep grief, that they are still yesterdaying.

You look away. You look down. They talk excitedly at each other, chirping like baby birds. As you quietly mourn your dwindling youth, they rave about a... well... rave they just attended in a former ice factory. You weren't aware they made ice in factories. You weren't sure where they made ice. You put your head in your hands and rub. As you ponder life's many injustices, the woman waxes poetic about an upcoming holiday to Georgia, where she'll stay in a "fruitarian free-love conscious chakra community".

"Amazing," the man says. "Like, totally."

You've always wanted to go to Georgia. You planned a trip, even. There was a Google Doc, you remember, but then… well… you know what happened.

Who happened.

You glance down at him in the buggy. He has collapsed, all the integrity gone from his spine. You scratch your elbow. As you think wistfully of suicide, the man and woman beside you discuss the myriad health benefits of licking poisonous Peruvian tree frogs.

Your baby stirs, lifting his head, teddy ears poking up, then cries. You shouldn't have sat down. That was another gamble. Another mistake. He likes to be pushed. He likes to be in motion, always. Fast stride. You know that. You tip your head back and curse those same fickle heavens.

You must push.

Push.

Always be pushing.

But you are so very, very tired. You unstrap him, pick him up, and chuck him over your left shoulder. The young people don't look, don't even glance at you, and why should they? Would you see you if you were them?

Of course not.

He normally loves this position, but today his wailing grows louder and louder. You feel his tears splash your shoulder, what will become another drool patch. The young couple gets up, perhaps annoyed by the decibels your infant son is reaching. They leave, walking past you, holding hands. You know, deep in your depths, that they're off to sex each other up. You sigh and, well, can find no way not to envy them.

!!!!!!!!!!!!!!!
!STOP, DAD!
!!!!!!!!!!!!!!!

For these paddling-pool shallow people, desperately licking yesterday's frog of hedonism, deserve only your pity and scorn. Look how they flail around trying to demarcate this day of late-stage capitalist consumption from yesterday's. Laugh at them, carpe diem-ing all over the place, dizzy from knocking their heads atop Maslow's so-easily-summited pyramid.

They are synthetic people, afloat at this early hour only because of synthetic substances. Holidaying at a Georgian fruitarian free-love conscious chakra community? Novelty's barrel is deep, yet they scrape its bottom. See how they must journey longer, party harder, imbibe stronger, and niche deeper just to get a kick. Any kick. They want firsts but the more they do, see, go, Insta, the further they must do, see, go, Insta.

Unlike you, Respected Sir.

For have you not found the answer? The solution? A way down off the pyramid?

You have: parenthood!

For what is that child, yelling and drooling into your shoulder, but the ultimate novelty machine?

Think about yesterday. It was around dusk. He was in the BabyBjörn swinging chair thing that he loves so much. You were singing your BabyBjörn song:

BabyBjörn
BabyBjörn
You are in the BabyBjörn
BabyBjörn
BabyBjörn
You are in the BabyBjörn.

Then his mother—the woman formerly known as your lover, now more of a roommate without benefits—came in holding a bright blue spoon with an elephant on it. On that spoon was a small piece of mashed banana.

"We're doing it," she said. "He's trying his first-ever bite of food."

"Epic," you said, scrambling to your feet. You then watched as your son considered the spoon, pondered it, BOOM—the spoon became a train, somehow.

"Choo-choo," Mama said, and then your son opened his mouth, didn't he? His little lips shook as he took of the banana mash. He closed his mouth. Paused. Went cross-eyed (you should really get that checked out). And then his face ripped into a wide smile.

Synapses snapped together.

There was love.

There was ecstasy.

IT IS TOO MUCH AND YET I REQUIRE MORE, his expression said, his tiny mind blown to smithereens. He did his trademark happy dance; the dance you love so much. That wriggle of hips and legs, like a beetle on its back trying to get out of a deep groove. It was magical. It was wondrous. It was everything. It was a first. Another first. And since you're so tethered to him emotionally, you lived that first with him, vicariously. It made you so giddy you had to sit down. Such a special moment, never to be repeated. And you were there, in the front row.

Today—barely an hour young—and yet you've already seen a human wear jeans (adorably tiny jeans) for the first time. Think about that. Jeans. And you were there. You put those jeans on him, even. Just about. Slowly. With a lot of cursing and while marvelling at how they'd bothered to sew in incredibly minuscule pockets, not even big enough for a coin. You tried it. Didn't fit. Then, barely a minute later, you saw a human get Marmite dropped on his new jeans... for the first time! Then you heard him say "Gagagook".

Gagagook!

FOR THE FIRST TIME.

The young people turn right, exiting the park.

"It's okay, hunny," you say. "Papa's here. Papa wants to be here." You lower him into the buggy. "I'll push," you say, as you strap him in and fast stride the first lap.

"There will be so many more," you say. "We're so lucky, you and I."

An Index of Things You Cared About Before Having a Child

Bed, softness.
Chocolate, organic-fair-trade-premium-picture-of-happy-cocoa-farmer-on-back.
Climate, change.
East, Middle.
Fashion, boldness.
Fashion, flattering of hippo hips.
Fashion, recency.
Food, freshness.
Food, novelty.
Food, nutritiousness.
Football, five-a-side.
Friendships, platonic.
Furniture, mid-century.
Games, computer.
Games, word.
Justice, social.
Mortality, yours.
Novelty, novelty.
Oboe, Japanese.

Opinions, people's of you.
Opinions, yours of people.
Orgasms, quality.
Orgasms, quantity.
Partner, romantic.
Patriarchy, smashing.
Pillow, firmness.
Pleasure, earned.
Pleasure, guilty.
Politics, leftie.
Restaurant table, best available based on complex but inarticulable personal methodology.
Room, ceiling height.
Room, furniture.
Room, lighting.
Room, loudness.
Room, size.
Sex, duration.
Sex, frequency.
Sex, novelty.
Sex, quality.
Sofa, plumpness.
Tribe, membership.
Youth, flaunting.

An Index of Things You Care About After Having a Child

Child, yours.
Chocolate, any.
Partner, life.
Silence, duration.
Sleep, quality

Be Careful What Your Kid Wishes For

There's a rare condition called De Clérambault's syndrome, or erotomania. Sufferers fall maddeningly, overwhelmingly, debilitatingly in love with someone in an instant. In the wonderful book *The Incurable Romantic*, by Frank Tallis (which explores love as a mental illness, a sympathetic position for parents), there's a chapter about a woman anaesthetised by her dentist.[1] They aren't close, she and the dentist. Not friends. Definitely not more than friends. Occasionally he looks in her mouth for money, but it's not a monogamous relationship. He does this with hundreds of people. He's just her dentist. Until she comes to from the anaesthesia after a routine operation and imprints on him, in a moment, in a flash, with devastating intensity.

The love she feels for him, she decides, is completely incomparable to the love she possesses for her husband, with whom she has had, by all accounts, a very pleasant twenty-year marriage. She is convinced the dentist loves her in just the same, all-encompassing way, yet he won't show it.

If anything, he seems weirded out by her.

Asks her to leave.

She begins stalking him.

He takes out a restraining order.

It doesn't help. She will not be restrained.

Eventually, he moves away. That helps, a bit. Life moves on, just about.

It's serious De Clérambault's syndrome. And it turns out, infants are prone to something like it. They too imprint on things and love them deeply, and sometimes inappropriately.

Evelyn has friends whose infant son imprinted on a lemon. You read that right. A lemon—the waxy yellow fruit. One day, when he was about six months old, he picked one up and decided, there and then, he'd never be without a lemon again. The good thing about lemons, I suppose, is that they're four for a euro, so you can easily swap them out while the child is sleeping. The bad thing about lemons, I suppose, is that they're lemons. You have the Lemon Kid. There will be looks, jokes about how if life gives you the Lemon Kid, at least you can make *him* make the lemonade.

Runa caught De Clérambault's syndrome too. We had a bunch of cuddly toys in her crib. Mostly, they'd been gifted to us. Some were the same plush toys of Evelyn's childhood, mottled but drenched in nostalgia. They were all there, in a pile. She had shown no preference for any of them. Until one day.

She was lying on her back and I was jiggling the toys over her, in turn. I held up a small grey monkey that my mother had given us. Runa stopped. Her blue eyes widened. Existence, previously confusing and multifaceted, collapsed into a single desire: Monkey.

She reached up for it and silently vowed she would never, ever let it go. Monkey—she never gave it a proper name—became her everything. She wouldn't leave the house without it. She barely moved around within the house without it clutched tightly to her chest. They were a team: Runa and Monkey.

Monkey would be there the first time she ate, crawled, walked. Monkey witnessed it all, the same wide, cheeky smile on its fluffy grey face. If I'd known about De Clérambault's syndrome before Monkey, I would have made sure every plush toy in her room was widely commercially available. Because what if she lost Monkey one day? We had some close calls. People chasing us out of shops holding Monkey aloft because it had tumbled unseen out of the buggy. I could have tongued those people deeply in the mouth. They didn't know how much heartbreak they had spared us (and Runa).

For a while, late at night, I scoured the Internet's darkest, plushiest corners, but without success. Monkey had been long discontinued.

Manias can end, or shift, as suddenly as they start. To secure backup, my mother posted on a lost-toy forum and a nice man replied and said he had Monkey too. The same Monkey. His son had imprinted on it as well, carried it everywhere until he was two years old. He was four now and didn't need Monkey anymore. The man sent it to my mother. The price he charged, I thought, was egregious, but we'd have paid ten times as much, that's how important Monkey was to our family. The man had us over a barrel, and he knew it.

Still, I hoped his child developed a lazy eye.

When it arrived, it wasn't the same Monkey. It was maybe 33 percent bigger, this Imposter Monkey. And the colour was off. The eyes were darker and more malevolent. For some reason, rather than keeping this fraudulent monkey in reserve, in case we lost the real McCoy, my mother, never much burdened by logic, showed it to Runa when we visited her in England.

Upon seeing it, Runa cocked her head and stared, silently forced to recalibrate to a new reality with multiple Monkeys.

Then she reached out a hand for it. "Mmmmm," she said, because she couldn't say "monkey" yet, and then she threw the actual Monkey, the real Monkey, her most loyal companion, her truest friend, her Everything, onto the cold kitchen floor. It stayed there for several days. Just before we left, I picked it up and stuffed it into the bottom of the suitcase. I could have sworn its smile had narrowed.

Little Monkey, as the true, authentic Monkey is now known, lives in the bottom drawer in Runa's room. It means nothing to her. I take it out sometimes and cuddle it. Big Monkey, the two-bit hustler, the scam simian, the chimpy charlatan, looks at me funny. Mockingly, almost, because he knows his position is secure.

For now.

Sleep Regression

Evelyn found me in the bedroom. Touched me on the shoulder. I stirred and realised I'd slept on the floor next to the cot. The night had passed in a blur. I looked down. My duvet was a jumper. My pillow was a plush pony. I wore drool like a beard. My breath was a war crime.

It had been my night.

"What happened?" she asked.

"She was up like fifteen times," I said. "It made no sense to keep going back to our bed."

"Teething, I guess?"

I yawned. She recoiled. It was the breath. "Probably," I said. "Something was up."

"Why didn't you bring her to our bed?" she asked.

"It was better one of us got some sleep."

My friend Manuel's phrase, *"You're only in the trenches for the first year"* came to mind. How much of the first year was left? Six months. Ouch.

Evelyn bent down, kissed me on the forehead; her breath smelt of toothpaste. "Sleep regressions are a bitch," I said. It had been nearly a week now. The nights awful. Runa was taking ages to go down; it seemed as if she were scared of sleep. She woke up a lot too, couldn't be soothed, always needed one of us in with her.

"It's just a phase," she said. "It'll pass."

"I know," I said, because there had been so many phases already. Everything was just a phase. I was just a phase. Humans were just a phase. Phases were just a phase, presumably.

Parenting's phases are so notable only because they're so short—before you know it, you're giving away your favourite romper with the little fish on it, now far too small, packing away the breast pump, and selling the baby bath at a flea market.

You celebrate the end of every phase, but there's sadness too.

"Coffee?" she asked.

"You bet."

Ten minutes later Runa was awake, and I carried her through to our bedroom. Evelyn's parenting shift was about to begin. "I think there's been another upgrade," I said, because she was noticeably more alert. It was as though she were seeing the room for the first time. Her eyes, which had previously skated from thing to thing, rarely focusing, now locked onto every object. Before we had a baby, I'd assumed they grew smarter linearly, a bit more each day. This isn't true. It's more like they go to bed one night and, during their sleep, get their mental firmware upgraded. They wake up as different people, loaded with new skills and abilities.

It's jarring. Suddenly they can roll. Or grasp things (literally). Respond to blue. Have a profound love of dogs. Giggle at Humpty Dumpty. Sit up, unaided. Imprint on a plush monkey. Crawl. Say "Mama". Say "Nana". Use the past tense.

It is miraculous each time, each jump, each upgrade, even if it's combined with one of the dreaded sleep regressions.

"She's awake," I said. "She's in the game now, for real."

"Yes," Evelyn said.

I went and cleaned my teeth.

There's a lot of disagreement about exactly when sleep regressions happen. Every child is different, but broadly speaking, you can expect them at four months, six months, eight months, twelve months, eighteen months, and two years old[1]. They usually last about two weeks. Those weeks are hard. Go easy on each other.

Part Three
Six to Twelve Months
- Just Parents

Gardens

Looking up from the corner of the bar, Kindle in my hand, I saw my friend Nick, fifteen minutes late, as usual. He'd just returned from England. His son, Tom, was two years older than Runa. Two and a half to her half. I raised my fist for a bump. He ignored it and, shoulders downturned, radiated glum.

"What's up?"

"I don't want to be here," he said, sitting down.

"Why didn't you cancel, then?"

"No," he said, tutting. "Berlin, I mean."

"Why?"

"No garden."

"What does that matter?"

"It doesn't matter to you—you've got a baby. I've got a toddler."

"How long have you lived in Berlin with no garden? Ten years?"

"Seven. Didn't matter then, did it?"

"But there are so many parks."

The beers I'd ordered for us arrived. He sipped from his

then frowned, as if it weren't wet enough. "It all changes," he said, ominously. "You ever go back to your hometown?"

"Did you know Hitler blew his up?" I said. "Let them use it for target practice?"

Nick laughed. "Braunau am Inn." Nick liked pub quizzes. "I wouldn't blow mine up. Just had a lovely few weeks there. Yeah, it all changes."

"You keep saying that. What changes, though?"

"Before, I had this really interesting life," he said, wistfully. "I travelled the world. Lived in half a dozen countries, didn't I? Now, I look at my sister, who's been nowhere, returned straight home after uni, took a job working with my mum, married her first serious boyfriend, bashed out three kids, bought a modest house, with a garden, just up the road from where we grew up, and I think, 'You lucky bugger. I want three kids. I want a garden.'"

"You didn't even want one kid until it happened."

"I didn't know how great it was then, though, did I? It all changes."

"Does it change for the better, though, Nick?"

"It does if you have a garden. My mum has a cracking garden. At 7am, the door swings open. Tom's poodling in and out. No flower on earth is watered more than a grandparent's flower when the grandkids are over." He cleared his throat. "Here, I have to carry him down four flights of stairs, wrestle him through the trash and rats of the courtyard, then bike five minutes through car-infested streets to a park full of even more trash and rats. There's the odd tree, sure." He shrugged. "I guess."

"But you live on the second floor?"

He paused. "I want a garden. A garden is 70 percent of parenting."

The Messy Middle

You and the kid are in the garden. You're pushing her on the baby swing. It's scary how much she loves the baby swing. Sometimes she stays in it so long she pukes. You've been pushing her for a long time, perhaps forever, even? The routine of it grinds your gears. You feel restless. This day is banal. This day is pointless. You want this day to end.

Your daughter swings closer, you push, she swings further away. "Waahahaha," she says.

Your daughter swings closer, you push, she swings further away.

Your daughter swings closer, you push, she swings further away.

Your daughter swings closer, you push, she swings further away. "Grgrggrggrggr," she says.

A great emotion, you decide. Yeah, that's what will elevate

this mediocre nothing of a day. Doesn't have to be a positive one. A negative one will do just fine, too. The important thing is its grandeur. Needs to be big enough to get lost in. The encompassing needs to be all, needs to be total. You try to remember if your partner has done something annoying lately? Or the neighbours? They were loud last night. They are very prone to Adele. You could go round, blow up in their faces? Or you could call someone and shout at them? The broadband provider? Rip into them about the speed during peak hours? You couldn't even masturbate properly the other day. Yeah, you could really give 'em hell.

Your daughter swings closer. "Mmmmrmrmsmammama-mam," she says.

Your daughter swings closer, you push, she swings further away.

Your daughter swings closer, you push, she swings further away.

Your daughter swings closer, you push, she swings further away.

Your daughter swings closer, you push, she swings further away.

You try on great regret but it doesn't fit. What should you regret? Your daughter? Why? It's not her fault, you bastard. And anyway, what's wrong with this frightfully ordinary moment? With being in the garden with your daughter, pushing her on the swing?

Your daughter swings closer, you push, she swings further away. Closer, then further away. She says nothing at all.

Parenting's always depicted in the books and on the TV shows as either amazing or terrible. The truth is different, you now know. Yes, parenting can be great, and yes, it can also be terrible, but both are fleeting states. Most of parenting, like the bulk of life, takes place in a Messy Middle. Not really much of anything, really. The cynically minded might say the Messy Middle is just killing time. Those of a more neutral persuasion, which you try to be, prefer the verb *passing*—passing time until the next feed, until the next nap, until shift change, until bedtime, until the weekend. It's not bad, the Messy Middle. It's just… messy; shapeless and undefined. It's what you make of it. It's your whole life, mostly.

Your daughter swings closer, you push, she swings further away. "Mmmmrmrmsmammamamam," she says.

Your daughter swings closer, you push, she swings further away.

Your daughter swings closer, you push, she swings further away.

Your daughter swings closer, you push, she swings further away. She looks at you and smiles.

You stamp your foot. *The best of it*, you decide. *I'm going to make the best of it.* Your daughter swings closer, then further away. Closer, and then, as she rises towards you, you stick out your tongue and push, harder this time. "You're going to space," you say. "Hold on tight."

117

The One Trait

It was raining, but we ignored that as we sat on our picnic blanket at the open-air Kinder Rave. There were at least fifty people around us in a clearing in the woods, glow-sticks in the air, channelling a time past but not necessarily better—when raving involved trying to charm your way through surly bouncers into packed clubs, where it mattered who you knew, what you wore, how you moved.

At the Kinder Rave, very little mattered. Kids speckled in glitter and with their faces painted as lions and monkeys grooved to melodic house music, having a blast. It was just Runa and me. Our picnic blanket was next to a man called Spark, his wife Libra, and their daughter Locus. It was all very Berlin, and so, ridiculous. Locus was maybe six months old, and yet Spark introduced the three of them as an "artist family." Spark had a habit of quoting Jordan Peterson, but that's not what this story is about.

It's about Libra's friend, Rainy, and yes, I'm still being serious about the names. Rainy had forgotten her blanket and so was sharing mine. Rainy's daughter was about six months old, two behind Runa, sitting up but not more. Runa

118

was in a brightly coloured zip-up unicorn suit eating a coconut snack bar and taking breaks to climb all over me, using me as her personal playground, as usual.

It was nice. It was fun. Runa was getting so much more interactive. I removed her from my head just as Spark dropped another Jordan Peterson "truth bomb".

Throughout our conversation, which, come to think of it, was just a Spark monologue, I'd seen Rainy watching Runa and me. Eventually it went quiet, or maybe I'd just finally learned how to tune Spark out.

"Can I ask you something?" Rainy said.

"Sure."

"How much time do you spend with your daughter?"

"Fifty percent." My chest inflated. I was a Modern Father.

She nibbled her bottom lip. "My boyfriend," she said. "He... well... he doesn't do much with our daughter. Like, well, on his own." She looked away, then back. "*Ever*. He says it's because he's an introvert, right, while I'm an extrovert. So, time with the baby is extra tiring for him and he needs breaks to recover. With me being an extrovert, I don't need breaks."

My mouth fell open. My tongue flopped out.

"Do you think that's true?" she asked.

I looked down at Runa and then up at Rainy. "I don't want to be harsh," I said. "Because, obviously, I don't know your partner. And I've been accused of being blunt. I once did a past-life-regression workshop, like a kind of meditation thing? It was me and a potbellied, monobrowed Australian investment banker. We did the meditation part and channelled into our former lives and all that. I saw nothing, just black, but this other guy, he said that he saw he was, in a former life, Helen of Troy."

I could see Rainy was growing confused about the relevance of this anecdote. "Anyway," I continued. "What you've just told me is *even more* ridiculous than that."

"Oh," she said. "Right."

She began to cry, which was regrettable. I thought about hugging her, but Runa freaked out if I touched anyone else, even her mother. She was a jealous kid. Fortunately, Libra, if that really was her name, noticed her friend's distress and scooted over and wrapped her in a hug.

"It gets better," I said. I meant looking after a child, of course, not things with her partner. The latter would stay just as crummy because, regardless of whether he was an introvert, he was a dick.

I thought back to the conversation I'd had on a boys' night out shortly after Runa was born. My friend Paul, another new dad, had said he wished he'd prioritised sleep genes in his choice of partner. He'd asked me what I would prioritise now I knew what it was like to have an infant, but I'd had no answer to the question. Listening to Rainy, I suddenly knew that I did...

Dating is an enormous part of our pre-parent lives. I have one friend who's been on a hundred dates. She has a spread-sheet. Keeps a public survey for people who want to date her to fill out. Another friend is addicted to Tinder. He spends over two hours a day hunting for new women and always casts them aside when he finds one minor flaw in them, as if there were none in himself.

If we know we want children, if we know we're on arcs that bend towards family, it's logical that we're testing parenting compatibility with everyone we date. Since Runa was born, a lot of people have asked me how I knew Evelyn was the right person with whom to procreate. Some have asked if, knowing what I know now, from the other side, all eight months of it, I'd pick her again?

Yes, I would.

And not because she smells nice and is stunning and intimidatingly intelligent and emotionally mature. Those things matter, sure, but in this period of our lives, they matter least.

No, I would pick her again because Evelyn is very sensitive to unfairness and injustice. In this first year of parenting, wonderful but also hard, exhausting, and monotonous, it hurts her to think she's not pulling her weight. Because of this, I know she's always calculating in her mind how much she does. She polices herself, as I police myself, because I'm also sensitive to unfairness. Which means we don't have to police each other. Which means we don't try to come up with ridiculous reasons the other should do more, like Rainy's boyfriend.

How much does unfairness hurt your partner? Will they fight to inconvenience themselves to help you? That's an excellent trait to look for. If you have that, if you're both doing that, you have a good chance because in that kind of relationship, it will be hard for resentment to fester and become the mould that will poison your shared lives.

I'm not saying it's enough. I'm just saying it's a good place to start.

Parenting Parity

It's an early hour. It's an ungodly hour. Scratching roughly at your shoulder, you enter the kitchen. She's there, your partner, the ying to your family's yang, on the chair, legs spread, mouth turned down, imitating a plane as she feeds your distracted child cereals.

"Hi, you two," you say, as you slope to the automatic coffee machine you recently purchased, the most expensive acquisition since the buggy. It was a whimsical decision made after a great day with friends. The mood was high. You were both Positive and had even had a glass of wine each. There was light hugging. Possibly a stroke of a buttock; you can't quite remember. You push the top left button on the machine—for cappuccino—and it whirs and gurgles and does everything else.

All of it.

Promptly.

Without complaint.

Or resentment. If only there were an Automatic Parenting Machine, you think. You could push a peekaboo button and it would keep your child quiet and, ideally, in another room.

You take your cup and sip. It is excellent. Foam warms your top lip. You feel much better after the thirty-minute nap you just took. It'll be her turn now. You'll finish the breakfast shift. You imitate a plane better than she does, anyway. Her engine sound has no depth; it's all *putt putt putt*.

"You're twenty minutes over," she says.

"What?" You look at the clock on the oven. *Shit.* You've over-napped.

"We had a deal," she says.

You look down into your coffee. "Sorry."

"I'm too awake now."

"Just lie down and stare at your phone, then?"

"No," she says, and with a sinking feeling, you realise she might be Negative. This is terrible news. "You're stuck with crabby me." Yes, this confirms it. She's Negative. It's not fair of her to claim Negative just because you slightly over-napped, something for which you're more than willing to reciprocate.

For if she's Negative, you must be Positive. You don't know if you can be Positive today, if you can play cheer-leader but Parenting Parity requires it. There can't be two Positives—that leads to dangerous, unsustainable exuberance and reckless, perhaps even deadly eye-off-the-ball, not to mention rash, decision-making (financially crippling holi-days, fully automated coffee machines, or, worse, second children).

Two Negatives? Well, that would be equally disastrous. Hopelessness stops time. You'd both be left in an endless, gaping, wretched moment that you'd have to fill with a midlife crisis, a substance-dependence issue, or an affair with a neighbour.

No, parity is better. Reversion to the emotional non-mean. For every couple, the number is different. For you two, neutral is about 6.5 out of 10 on the happiness scale.

That works.

That's sustainable.

You sip your coffee. It really is excellent. More foam sizzles on your upper lip. You lick it, turn, smile, and make your voice surge upwards. Pep, they call it. "Take two hours," you say. "Just for you, my darling. And since it's the weekend and the forecast is good, how about we go to the zoo this afternoon?" You bend down. "Would you like to go to the zoo, honey?"

"Oooh oooh," your child says, making their monkey noises.

Mama scowls. Mama doesn't want to go to the zoo. Mama suffers and wants, in turn, to make suffering. "Come on," you say. "We can stop at that Ethiopian place you love afterwards? Where you eat the big edible plate?"

"Hmm," she says, because she really does love that Ethiopian place. "It's called an injera. And it's not a plate. It's insensitive to call it a plate. Why are you always so insensitive to other cultures?"

"Sure," you say. "Right. My treat."

"Maybe," she concedes, because it's expensive, that place, bearing in mind they don't even have plates to wash up.

"Oooh, oooh, ahhhhh," your child says, hitting a plastic spoon against their head. Delight and Coco Pops spray around the room.

You wonder how it will be when your child is older. Whether Family Parity will replace Parent Parity. Three pronged, not two. You hope your child will be mostly Positive. Melancholy suits you and her mother better. Has more nuance to it. Not that you show that now, of course. No, you are Positive. You must be Positive. You click your fingers. "Mama, shower," you say. "Kid, let's get you out of that chair. You and I have a date with Bluey, then later, we're all off to the zoo."

"Fine," Mama says. "I guess."[1]

Sleep Training

It was so, so late. It was desperately, hopelessly late. It was at least 8pm, maybe even 8:30. My eyes no longer worked. Runa sprang up like a mushroom, holding onto the bars of her cot/baby prison to stand. I lifted my head from the back of the chair. "Runa," I grunted. "Sleep now. Or I'm leaving."

She started to dance.

"Runa," I barked. "Sleep."

Reluctantly, she lay back down. I looked surreptitiously at the phone I was holding at an odd angle, ankle height, so she couldn't see it and demand videos. I'd already been in the room for an hour. That was an hour I could have spent working, catching up with Evelyn, or sitting on the balcony staring forlornly into the middle distance, lightly ruing all I had become. Or, perhaps, would now not become.

Runa lobbed her dummy over the bars. It hit me on the nose. "Why you little—"

I pulled the spare dummy from my pocket, got up, and shoved it in her mouth. I sat back down in a huff. She knew the dummy made her sleep. That was why she'd thrown it so gleefully out. She hurled the new one out too, but the other way, against the wall, from where it fell down the small gap and then tumbled under her cot, where my fat arms couldn't reach.

It was a provocation.

An escalation.

A real show of force.

"Okay," I said. "That's it. I'm out. Good night." I got up and blustered out of the room.

Runa burst into emotional flames, howling and whining and screaming and being so, so devastated. She still never wanted to be alone. Not even for a minute.

I ignored her cries and walked to the living room.

"Going well?" Evelyn asked, over the sounds of Runa's suffering.

"I can't do this anymore," I said. "I can't lose one and a half hours of my evening just waiting for her to sleep."

"We could sleep train?" Evelyn said. "I think she's ready."

"What's sleep training?"

Evelyn got up, found the chapter in Emily Oster's *Cribsheet*, her bible, handed me the book, and then went to console Runa. I sat down and read it. I liked what it said.

Sleep training. Yes. We were doing it.

Sleep training is controversial in parenting circles. Not breastfeeding controversial, but up there. As a Modern Father, though, you know other people's opinions can't hurt you and that Total Family Happiness is the metric by which you make decisions. Much of which depends on sleep. We've covered all this already. Knowing that, and if your infant falls asleep as slowly and with as many shenanigans as ours, sleep training becomes a must.

What is it?

Well, it's gradually (or not so gradually) teaching your child to soothe themselves to sleep and then back to slumber should they wake up during the night, without needing your presence. Research shows that sleep training leads to improved sleep consolidation, meaning infants sleep for longer stretches. A review by a task force appointed by the American Academy of Sleep Medicine found that sleep training "produces reliable and durable changes in bedtime problems and night wakings in infants and young children. An overwhelming majority of children respond favourably to these behavioural techniques, resulting in not only better sleep, but also improvements in child and family well-being".[1]

There are several established methods, and in this case, I see no reason to rail against the establishment. Let's review the most common ones.

1. The cry it out, or extinction, method

This method involves putting your baby down in their crib, saying goodnight, and then walking away, not to return, even if they cry. Same if they wake during the night.

Pros: It's effective; babies quickly learn to fall asleep on their own.

Cons: You are likely to feel quite monstrous. Some babies become increasingly stressed out or anxious from prolonged crying, winding themselves up and up, before your heart eventually breaks and you go comfort them, which takes ages. This method requires a chill baby.

2. The Ferber method, or graduated extinction

This method involves putting your baby down to sleep, allowing them to cry for a predetermined amount of time, then comforting them; e.g. four minutes out of the room, one minute in the room consoling, then repeat. You then gradually increase the time between checks each day.

Pros: It's gentler than the extinction method, and many parents find it easier to tolerate, since they get to go in and comfort their baby periodically.

Cons: You need to be disciplined to stick to the intervals. Also, some babies become more agitated by the periodic check-ins, each reanimating them rather than making them sleepy.

3. The chair, or no-tears, method

This method involves sitting in a chair next to your baby's crib or bed. You wait until they sleep, then, each day, you edge the starting position of the chair further away, until you're out of the room entirely.

Pros: Gentle. Low stress, and likely a low number of tears, too.

Cons: Time-consuming.

If you pick 1 or 2, in those blocks of time where you can't comfort them, you'll hate yourself, life, the universe, and sleep training. You will feel like a scoundrel, which doesn't mean you are one. Keep reminding yourself of the bigger picture—Total Family Happiness and your child's learning the important skill of self-soothing.

Whichever method you pick, combine it with a rock-solid, reliable, tediously familiar bedtime routine. Sleep is a habit; the body learns to be tired at the same time each day, and to adjust its sleep rhythms to the expected duration of slumber. Don't think of this project as just sleep training your child but also as the first part of a sleep routine for you.

A few minutes later, Evelyn walked back into the room. "She's down."

I closed the book. "Thanks," I said, because it was my night to put Runa to bed, so Evelyn had just done a tiny amount of overtime.

"What do you think?" Evelyn asked.

Suddenly, Runa wailed. We crumpled. It wasn't over.

I handed her the book and got up. "We start tomorrow."

"I don't know if I'm ready," Evelyn said.

"This is her fault. She's making us do this."

"She's a baby."

"You're a baby. Toughen up. We're sleep training."

If one of you is particularly sensitive to the sounds of your infant's suffering, it's best that the person goes out for the night. It's going to be rough. It took forty-five minutes of five-minute rounds before Runa was so exhausted from crying that she fell asleep. But then something magical happened: there were half as many rounds on day two, and on day three, she didn't cry at all, had simply accepted that she now accompanied herself to sleep.

It felt like a miracle.

It didn't last forever. You'll have to sleep train several times, usually because children get sick and when they're sick, all bets are off—they need different things. More closeness, more comfort. We'd usually just sleep in her room with her, alternating nights of miserable sleep on the spare mattress by her bed.

Then we'd sleep train again. And it worked. It's amazing.

Egg

"It's five years," you say. You're at an Italian restaurant. Your son is in a high chair splatting French fries. The staff keeps coming out to play with him.

"It's six," your lover says.

"We met in 2018."

"It was 2017."

Doubt creeps in; you're notoriously bad with dates. "Was it?"

"I always count the photos in the kitchen," she says. You get hipster photo-booth pictures taken each anniversary.

"Maybe we missed a year?" you ask.

She shakes her head. "It's the only ritual we have. We didn't miss a year. It's six years."

"Hmm," you say, thinking about how, in the Before Times, you used to poll your relationship every fifteen minutes: Was something off? Were your feelings for each other changing? Was compatibility slipping? How could you turn things around? A game night? A weekend away? Two hallowed words: *city* and *break*.

She did this too, you could tell. And why not? You had the

time to probe into the smallest minutia of your emotions, and of your days. Your patience with each other was limitless. If you were in the same room, some part of you was always touching.

It was glorious.

Now, here you are, in both this restaurant and the After, having somehow, maybe, lost an entire year of your love. You try to remember when you last polled the relationship. When you last touched. Wasn't there a quick hallway hug around Monday lunchtime?

Maybe.

"Waahwaahaaahhhhhhh," the kid says.

Post-baby, it's hard not to look at your once-thunderous love—that you used to hear in every song, feel in every caress —and think, *Yeah, it has shrivelled somewhat.*

You put down your knife and fork, sip your soda, and caution yourself. One must be realistic. There are only so many hours in the day; only so much energy in your bodies. You are often in the same room, but your minds are elsewhere—in the past, in the future, in sleep, in fear, in banality, in TikTok.

That's understandable. Your sex life is nonexistent, but why wouldn't it be?

"Mamamamamammamama," the kid says. Your partner reaches over and wipes some drool from his mouth. The kid is always on you. It's no surprise that by the time he's finally down, docile in his cot, you're touched out. No longer craving intimacy, you crave autonomy. You end each day in the same bed as your partner, but you aren't yourselves there. You are containers. Empty vessels. The bed is just where you go to charge yourselves, like you do with your phones on the bedside tables.

"Mamamamamammamama," the kid says, still splatting. Before he can knock the plate over the side of the high chair, you move it back to the centre, thinking about American schools and how they used to give kid-couples an egg. Both would sign its shell and, in doing so, become responsible for keeping it alive for a week, passing it back and forth. It was supposed to show them how much responsibility it is to have a baby.

The experiment is wrong, you think. The egg is not the baby. Babies aren't fragile. The egg is the love the parents share. That's what's endangered when a couple has children. That's the thing they have to protect. The thing that hunger, fear, sadness, anxiety, sleep deprivation, routine, and logistics keep trying to splat, as your baby does his fries.

It's hard protecting that love. It's hard not forgetting that love. It's hard not doubting that love. You take another sip of soda and look up at your life partner, slurping spaghetti.

Faith, my paramour.

Have faith that what you're sowing today, you'll harvest later—together. That large bounties are yet due to you. That one day, your love will thunder and roar through the valley of your lives once again.

It is six years, you realise. She's right. She's always right. There will be many more; you will make it so.

"What are you thinking about?" she asks.

"Nappies," you say. "We shouldn't forget to pick up nappies on the way home."

"Sure," she says. "Okay."

Sleeping Through

I crawled up a long tunnel in my mind and emerged in my bed, tongue twice its usual thickness. I rubbed my eyes and cursed a world I knew would need, want, and demand things from me. Weak winter light slid between the cracks in the blue curtains and, instinctively, I grasped bleary-eyed for my phone, hoping there might be an e-mail that changed everything.

The display revealed it was 7:30am. Later than usual. Later than I would have guessed.

Also, my eyes... working quite well.

And my arm—which put the phone down after I'd found only spam, newsletters I'd forgotten signing up for, and four e-mails for other Adam Fletchers sent to me in error—felt light and springy. Not as if it had been carrying a baby around all night. I turned to Evelyn, who was deep into her phone.

"Did she wake up in the night?" I asked.

She didn't turn from the screen. "You went in, didn't you?"

"I... I don't think so, no?"

She lowered the phone. Turned. Scratched her head. "Did I, then?" There was wonder in her voice.

It wasn't always easy to remember who'd got up in the night to go into Runa's room because, when she wrenched us from sleep, we were muzzy and torpid. What we did in there —pick her up a bit, cuddle a bit, sing a bit, give milk a bit, put her down a bit, wait a bit—was so routine and tedious, there was nothing to remember. Yet, we often did remember, albeit hazily, even if it was just how long it took for us to go back to sleep. Something we would moan about over breakfast.

"I don't remember," I said.

"Maybe I got up?" Evelyn asked.

"I don't remember you getting up and I usually hear you because you refuse to step over that loud floorboard because you're a horrible person who hates me."

She blinked slowly. "I don't think I got up. Look if the milk bottle is next to her bed?"

I went and checked. We were groggy detectives trying to solve a non-crime. Runa was still sleeping, curled onto her side, one leg sticking through the bars of her baby prison.

"Nope," I said, smiling. "Can't have happened."

"Can't have happened," Evelyn agreed. "But that means...?"

I pumped the air with my fist. "She slept through."

"She slept through," Evelyn said.

I did a small jig, elbows out. "OH, HAPPY DAY," I sang.

"OH, HAPPY DAY," Evelyn echoed.

"OH, HAPPY DAY," we sang together.

It was the most euphoric I'd felt in a long time, perhaps since Runa was born. It was a glimmer of what was to come. A hint that our lives, or at least our sleep, might slowly become our own again.

"*OH, HAPPY DAY—*"

"Shhh," Evelyn said. "You might wake her up."

"Sleep training!" I whispered, flashing all my teeth.

She nodded. "Sleep training is the best."

Bath

My daughter was bathing on the balcony in the baby bath, a genius idea of mine. She was eight months old. Sat in there with two boats, a bubble-blowing whale, three cups, and a water pistol. She couldn't stop giggling.

"Ha-huh Ha-huh Ha-huh. Haha. Huh. Ha."

Something like that, anyway. Words could never do justice to the sound. I vowed to make it my ringtone. I was sitting nearby, but she didn't need me. Was lost to the moment. To the joy of bathing, al fresco. To water. To life.

She tipped the yellow cup over her head and giggled more. She threw it down. *Splash*. Giggled more. Picked it up. Giggled more.

"Ha-huh Ha-huh Ha-huh. Haha. Huh. Ha."

I had never witnessed joy so unbridled and pleasure so untrammelled.

"Ha-huh Ha-huh Ha-huh. Haha. Huh. Ha."

I shouted Evelyn's name.

"What?" she said, grumpily, because she suspected a task was imminent. It was not. She came, pulled in by the siren call of that giggle.

"Ha-huh Ha-huh Ha-huh. Haha. Huh. Ha."

She sat down next to me.

"Ha-huh Ha-huh Ha-huh. Haha. Huh. Ha."

"This is extraordinary," she said.

"She's having the best time."

Runa splashed, tried to use the water pistol, failed, ate it, threw it out. Giggled. "Ha-huh Ha-huh Ha-huh. Haha. Huh. Ha." Poured one cup into another. "Aahhahahahhaha," she said, like a good-hearted pirate, two grogs in.

"Ha-huh Ha-huh Ha-huh. Haha. Huh. Ha."

My cup filled all the way up. My cup runneth over. "That giggle," I said.

"Yeah," Evelyn said, slipping her arm over me, nuzzling in against my shoulder.

"I once drove seven hours to attend a concert," I said. "But I've never heard anything a tenth as good as that giggle."

"It's the best giggle," she agreed.

The giggling continued. "Ha-huh Ha-huh Ha-huh. Haha. Huh. Ha." She turned to us both and flapped her arms, her smile stretching to her ears. She had soap bubbles on her head and could have been the star of a no-tears shampoo commercial.

"She is spectacular," Evelyn said.

"Yes."

"We did good."

"That giggle," I said, again, because I wasn't ready to let it go.

"Yes."

"My heart," I said.

"Mine too."

The Nourishment of Nurture

You used to be the king of the world, didn't you? A law unto yourself. If, drunk on whisky, you wanted to set fire to five hundred dollars on a windy hill, at 4am, wearing just your underpants, only that old narc common sense could stop you.

Yeah, nothing mattered unless you said it mattered. You were judge, jury, and executioner—and you sentenced hedonistically.

It was, mostly, awesome.

But then, in your infinite but inscrutable wisdom, you had a child, didn't you? Or perhaps, even, several. And now you're a father, no longer the dead centre of your own private universe, the fulcrum by which everything can be moved. Now, you rarely get to do what you want; instead, you do what your child wants. Your autonomy has taken a colossal hit.

And your happiness will too, unless you learn to find it elsewhere, because as parents, we're paid differently by life. We become poor in autonomy—the ability to do what we want, when we want, with whom we want—so we must learn to value something else: transferred autonomy.

Transferred autonomy is the ability to give a loved one what *they* want, when they want it, with whom they want it. My mother, who strongly believes that "you're only ever as happy as your least happy child", transferred a huge amount of her autonomy to my two siblings and me.

Too much, probably. Why would she do that? Well, I think, while autonomy feels fantastic in the moment, if you take the time to watch the people you love flourish because of work you do—often thanklessly and behind the scenes— you realise transferred autonomy is actually the more satiating of the two. Self is sugar, transferred is salad: not sexy, not always what you crave, but what's good for you on a deeper level, over a longer time.

More nourishing.

Yes, it's a Saturday, yes, you could be down the pub, yes, the football is on. But you're not. You're here. You're in your living room with people who need you. See how they giggle when you jiggle them? How they grin as they eat the food you made them? How they clap as they (well, let's be honest, mostly you) complete the six-piece puzzle you bought them?

Clapping is new. You taught them clapping. That's a skill they'll have forever now. Oh, they fell over. Look how their little arms reach up for you, how their bottom lip trembles, how they turn to you for reassurance it's all going to be okay.

Your time will come again. Not today. Not even soon. But you will return, whisky splashed, to that hill. In the meantime, nourish your family, and let that nourish you.

Crawling

"She's doing it," Evelyn shouted.

"Doing what?" I asked, from Runa's room, where I was putting away socks, or rather, trying to—none of the damn socks, the ones she hadn't lost, matched. What kept happening to the socks? Were all socks in the world unique, like fingerprints?

"Get in here," Evelyn shouted again.

"What?" I shouted. "I'm socking in here. I hate socks. Or maybe socks hate me."

"She's mobile," she said. "She's crawling."

I threw all the socks in the air and ran towards the kitchen then skidded to a stop as a fast-moving object propelled itself towards me, on its front, stabbing its elbows into the ground and pulling all its weight forward, a look of steely determination on its face. "Runa Fletcher, reporting for duty, sir," the army-crawling object said, or would have, could she talk.

"Jesus," I said. "Just look at her go."

"I would," Evelyn said, between sobs. "But my eyes aren't

working." She blew her nose on some kitchen roll. "I'm so proud."

Runa, still elbowing the floor with great tenacity, reached my foot. She celebrated by biting it. "Hey, you little rug rat."

"Grgrgrgrgrgr," she said, but what she meant was, "Runa Fletcher, sir. Inspecting your floors, sir. Also partially cleaning the floors with my stomach, sir. Chewing your foot, sir."

I lowered myself to my knees. "Look at you. Wow. You're really doing it, you are."

"Out of my way, sir," she said.

"Okay, okay, fine, I'll move," I said, wiggling over so she could pass into the hallway.

"She's all grown up," Evelyn said, her voice squeaking. "It's happening so fast. Now she's crawling and soon she's going to be walking and then she'll be moving out and it'll be too—"

"Chill out, honey. It's only crawling. And barely even that. There's a long time from here to moving out. My brother didn't move out until he was thirty. Actually, he's not really even moved out now. Where do you think she's going?"

"She's going everywhere, of course. Wouldn't you?"

"Well," I said. "All the chocolate's in here, so strategically, she's blundered already. Do we need to go with her, you think?"

"What about the bathroom?" she said. "Did you babyproof the bathroom?"

"Yeah, a month ago, when she started rolling sideways everywhere, sort of, but mostly just with her head."

"The drunk-worm stage," she said, dabbing her eyes. "I don't remember that one from the books."

"No," I said. "That was her own thing."

Evelyn moved closer to the door. "I stopped taking her out. It was too embarrassing."

"Me too. I'm going after her."

"I'm coming. We need to make videos."

"We have so many videos."

She got out her phone to make more videos. We moved into the hallway. I slipped my arm around Evelyn and we cuddled as we watched Runa disappear into the distance, become a dot on the horizon—or so she would have, had we not lived in a piddly little shoebox apartment.

"She's mobile," I said, redundantly.

"It's incredible," Evelyn said. "No?"

"The puppet has become the puppeteer."

"What?"

Runa turned her head to check we were watching. I gave her a thumbs up. "Before, we had to puppet her, right? To take her everywhere she wanted to go. Now she can take herself. The puppet is puppeteering itself."

"She's not a puppet."

"You called her a drunk worm."

"I'm her mother."

"What difference does that make?"

She didn't answer. Runa swung a left into her bedroom.

"What's the next stage?" I asked.

"On the knees."

"She'll crack that by the weekend," I said proudly.

"She'll crack that by tonight," Evelyn said. "I'm going to go buy some more tissues."

There are approximately six stages to crawling. Here's a brief guide to their many delights.

Step 1 – Head up (0–7 months)

They'll only be able to lift their head a few precious seconds at first. They'll get frustrated. Let them struggle. Propping them under a cushion can be good, so they're not completely flat and have a better view. Flashing lights can help. You want to stimulate them so they hate tummy time less.

At some point, they'll go from being able to lift their head to being able to sort of prop themselves up on their hands. Their neck will be long. They will give off serious turtle vibes. They will hate tummy time less. Sometimes they'll do a really cute swimming motion while lying on their bellies.

Step 2 – Rolling over (4–6 months)

This is an exciting stage. They can now go from A to B, sort of, sideways. They probably won't, though, because at first, they'll only know how to roll from back to belly or belly to back, which are different skills, weirdly.

Step 3 – Sitting up (5–7 months)

Here you'll really see them learning to balance and strengthening their core. It's hard to know for whom it's more thrilling: you or them. They might even turn in a circle, or pivot back down onto their front. At this point they're basically mobile, using a variety of all the previous skills together in a hotchpotch, inefficient, devastatingly cute manner.

Stage 4 – Rocking and planking (6–8 months)

At this point they're getting their legs into the game, often dropping from a sit on their forearms into a sort-of press-up. The muscles (and muscle memory) of their legs aren't as developed as those of their arms, so they spend a lot of time rocking, building them up.

Stage 5 – Army crawl (7–9 months)

Now they're really putting it all together. There is forward, predictable motion. Where they look, they go, mostly using their arms to get there.

Stage 6 – Hands-and-knees crawl (7–10 months)

They're up. Their legs are doing half the work now. They're really scooting around. They will soon, like in a week, be scarily fast at this. It will shock you. It might even shock them. Your baby crawls. You will be so proud, as will they. If you didn't babyproof, babyproof. If you babyproofed, babyproof again.

The Playground

The front door opened. Evelyn breezed in, out of breath from the stairs, Runa balanced over her shoulder, babbling. Evelyn put her down and she crawled off towards a tennis ball, like a golden retriever.

"The playground," Evelyn said. I turned from making one of my epic salads. Runa was ten months old, and we were now regularly taking her to the playground, where she liked to sit in the sand and dig with her little shovel. "It's quite relaxing, somehow. Have you noticed?"

"Yes," I said, as I surgically sliced out the innards of a cucumber. "I think it's because men and woman are mixing but dating is off the table."

Her head tipped back slightly. "That's true. You don't need to be suspicious of anyone's motives. You can talk to anyone. *Huh.*"

"And," I said, buoyed by this clarity of observation, "there's also, like, absolutely nothing at stake, you know? Because we're parents and so, by default, we're lame."

Her nose wrinkled. "That's ridiculous."

"Wait until you taste this salad," I said. "It has three types of nuts. Now that's ridiculous."

I thought more about my Grand Unified Theory of Parental Lameness when I was next in the sandpit, part of a crescent of parents, our tote bags full of sand toys and snacks by our sides and our infants in front of us, climbing over each other like kittens in a sack. I felt very at peace, very calm, very sure I was right.

Runa took her small red shovel and splatted the sandcastle I had just made her. "Grrraahhahahhahha," she said, grinning. It was obvious she wanted me to make her yet another sandcastle.

"I've already made like four hundred."

She waved her shovel. "Grrraahhahahhahha."

"I feel like you don't understand how tedious this is for me? How Sisyphean?"

She stared up at me.

"Worse, even. He was on a mountain. At least he had a view."

"Grrraahhahahhahha," she said, flapping the shovel.

"Okay," I said. "Fine."

Anyway, the theory…

Humans are a status animal, and there's not much status in being like everyone else, so we're forced to specialise. As adults, we go to great lengths—in fact, it's kind of *the* great project of adolescence—to become individuals. To separate ourselves from the herd, whether with the sharpness of our intellect, the bulge of our biceps, the creativity of our tattoos, or the richness of our knowledge of Japanese oboe. We fan these unique interests, achievements, idiosyncrasies, anecdotes, and pedigrees wide to attract mates, like the peacock parades its tail feathers.

I'm not like the others, we broadcast. *Pick me.*

Then someone picked us, didn't they? And so ended our

Goldilocks search for someone who looked just right, smelt just right, loved just right, fucked just right. We had a child with that person, and now we're happy, as much as can be reasonably expected. And thus, we have retired from the great genetic pic "n" mix. The only dates in our future will be play dates with parents and children we meet at the playground.

We spend so much time there, it would be easy to resent it. To see only how lame it is. To bemoan the sheer ground-hoggedness of each afternoon there.

That would be wrong. For playgrounds are actually really special places that achieve something few others in life manage: they are genuinely egalitarian.

Because, while we adults are all proudly, stubbornly different, all two-year-olds are exactly the goddamn same. Want to climb the same climbing frames. Slide the same slides. Be helped across the same monkey bars. Bash other kids over the head with the same red plastic shovels. Cry in the same annoying way when they don't get the exact crisp they've decided they must have right now or the world will end. Giggle in the same delighted way as they splat the sand-castles their parent made for them fifty-seven times in a row.

And, in caring for them, we all become the same too. The guy across the sandpit, hair slicked back, could be a million-aire media mogul, an international playboy, the husband of his high-school sweetheart, a fugitive bank robber, an insur-ance salesman, a supermarket cashier, or the eminent world expert on Japanese oboe.

Doesn't matter. No one cares. He's shin deep in the pit, like us, shoes off, like us, dragging a purple starfish shape around, like us, has clothes speckled with vomit and poop and drool, like us. In a minute, he'll be pushing his kid on the swings, next to ours, making the same small talk about how his son's walking is/isn't going or about whether he's sleeping through the night yet. Outside of this place, he might have made quite a name for himself, but here, he doesn't even have one. He's just "Winnie's dad".

And that's because here, we are parents. Here, we are nothing. Equal; equally irrelevant.

And that's nice.

Playground Dads

My many, many hours on the playground have revealed that some men are, foolhardily, still playing the status game there and attempting to have unique fathering personalities. They fail because each falls into one of the following siring subtypes.

1. Macho, Macho Dad

Just because you've had a baby doesn't mean you have to compromise your rock-hard abs or grisly, far-off stare. *Macho, Macho Dad* proves you can provide while looking damn good doing it. Admire him now, as he engages in the roughest of rough play, casually lobbing his child in the air as if they're the set of keys to his Harley Davidson. He's not merely on the playground, like you; he *owns* it—king of the urban jungle.

Catchphrase: "Grrrrrrrrrrrrrrrrrrrrrrrrrrrrrr."

Most likely to be seen: Pushing a cluster of children aside so he can show them how you *really* fly the flying fox.

2. Earth Papa Eddie

Earth Papa Eddie is so, so nice. And so happy to see you. He always remembers your name. Uses it often, too, he does, as he sips from his flask of rose-infused kombucha tea, adjusts his moss-green cardigan, and tells you about his latest urban-bee-keeping experiments. In a dozen hours together, he's never asked a single question—about you, about your kid, about anything—because why would he? He already has all the answers. As he settles in for a long, meandering diatribe that will swerve across Big Pharma, Paganism, Seasteading, the Far Right, the Deep State, and Quiches, you look down at his son, not even two, dressed in a Peruvian poncho and digging in the sand as if trying to bury himself, and see cringe at the edges of his young eyes.

Catchphrase: "You use suntan lotion? We only use *natural* things on little baby Kigh." (It's pronounced Keegan.)

Most likely to be seen: Humming a Hawaiian ditty while he hands out homemade, gluten-free, additive-free, sugar-free, taste-free tempeh sticks.

3. Big Kid Billy

You never see *Big Kid Billy*, but he sees you. He sneaks in behind you and throws you in an affectionate headlock. "This guy," he shouts, then casts you aside to get down on the ground and fistbump your child. *Big Kid Billy* loves nothing more than being in the dirt with the kiddywinks, who flock to him as if he's the Pied Piper of Parenting. Everywhere he goes, kindergartens try to hire him. Parenting comes naturally to him because he's never grown up. Still collects comics. Loves every superhero franchise, especially, unfathomably, Ironman. In your best moments, you enjoy his pep and use him as free childcare. At your worst, you look at how he musters more enthusiasm for hide-and-seek on a wet November Tuesday than you've ever managed, even on your child's July birthday—and you hate him. Sometimes, you even hide from him, swerving off to a different playground when you see him racing other kids up the ladder of the pirate ship.

Catchphrase: "The best thing about being a dad? I think it's probably *everything*."

Most likely to be seen: Leading a conga line around the sandpit with a bucket on his head.

4. Competitive Claude

There are many reasons to have children: boredom, not wanting to break a multi-million-year genetic line, a desire to pay existence forward, intellectual curiosity, or, as is the case with *Competitive Claude*, to finally have someone to beat at football.

For him, everything is a competition. The world will never go easy on his children, so neither will he. That's why his family can never just go home—they always have to race there. Why he celebrates every goal, no matter how embarrassing the scoreline: 8–0, 9–0, 10–0; it doesn't matter to him—each is proof that he's still got it. That he's beating ageing.

Catchphrase: "Last one at the ice-cream shop gets nothing. Go!"

Most likely to be seen: Celebrating loudly, arms up in the air, T-shirt pulled over his head, imitating an airplane because he's scored another glorious free kick against his goalkeeping daughter, who can't even walk yet.

5. Part-Time Papa Pat

Part-Time Papa Pat is a magician with just one trick: making himself disappear. A spotting of him on the playground is a real collector's item. You never remember his name, but you know his ex-wife, Cindy, well. After all, she's here six days a week. *Part-Time Papa Pat* is only occasionally around, on Sunday afternoons, if the weather's good and there's no footie on. Hungover. He's always hungover. Each time here is like his first. He has none of your rich local-domain knowledge about where on the slide there's a sharp nick, or how that swing on the far left is a wonky deathtrap. His child, desperate for his attention, sticks to him like poop to a leg. "Dad, look at me. Dad, I'm up here. Dad, no, we still have more time. Dad, wait. Dad, come back."

Catchphrase: "Err, I don't know, kid, ask your mother?"

Most likely to be seen: Racing around town in his sports car, his new girlfriend (fifteen years his junior) riding shotgun.

6. Sad Dad Dave

A common playground sight, *Sad Dad Dave* keeps himself on the periphery, avoiding the eyes of the other dads. It's as if, by not engaging, he can convince himself he's somewhere else. Or more likely, some-*when*-else. He has only one expression—deep pinch. Great wafts of resentment, misery's cologne, emanate from him. He wears all black, as if in mourning. There are dark rings around his eyes. He sits on the furthest bench away, beneath the oak tree, silently counting down the years until he'll get his life back. What he doesn't know yet is he's lost it for good. He's chasing the shadows of who he once believed he was. Of a time when possibility quaked before him. Of a time when he was a DJ in Ibiza and the world danced to *his* tune. Of a time in which he only had to look at women and they moistened. Of a youth already spent.

His son calls out to him. He looks up slowly from his phone. His boy, in the Manchester United kit, waves frantically for his attention, proud to have summited the big slide, alone.

"That's... good, mate," he says, just about, the words tumbling like pebbles from his mouth.

Maybe he wanted this, but then it's easy to want something, isn't it, when you don't know its full size and scope? How it feels, how much it will take, and then you can't give it back. Does he want to give it back?

In this heavy moment, yes, he does. He loves his child, don't get him wrong, but he doesn't love being his child's parent.

Catchphrase: "Yeah, buddy, I'm watching. Nice one. Great. *Yeah.*"

Most likely to be seen: Glumly scrolling through photos of a lad's holiday nine years ago or swiping at a dating app, dreaming of having the affair that will make him feel what he used to—unencumbered and powerful, the protagonist in a great story yet unwritten, instead of the sombre side character in someone else's epic quest towards adulthood.

7. Workaholic Will

Workaholic Will, the big-time legal linchpin, blusters onto the playground still in his dress shirt and tie, a harried look on his face.

His son tries to drag him towards the seesaw. "I've just got to finish this call…" he says, covering the phone briefly; it's never out of his clammy hands.

His son dissolves like a newspaper in rain.

"No, I'll be there in a second, mate. No, *I will*. I just have to finish this call. It's important. And then an e-mail. A bit of spreadsheet, maybe. I know, *mate*, I know I said I'd have time today. And I will. And then we'll play football, yeah. I promise. I know I promised that yesterday, too. Well, I double promise then, okay? And anyway, you're four now—you don't want to play with your lame old dad, do you? Go play with those kids." He points at children who are nine, maybe even ten. They will eat his child as if he's frosted cereal. "Where's your football? Oh, bugger, I forgot it." He grabs the back of his neck with his free hand. A bead of sweat pools on his eyebrow. "Well, you rushed me here, didn't you? Oh… no… don't cry, love. No… come on. Don't be like that. You know Daddy's job is important. Why are you sobbing now? I'll be five minutes. Hey, how about you just take this money and buy yourself an ice cream, yeah? That okay? Cool. Take your time." He lifts his phone back to his ear. "Sorry, Brian, no, nothing important. So, about that meeting tomorrow, I really think the best strategy is…"

His parents should have called him *Won't*, you think, as you sit in silent judgement.

Catchphrase: "I know, I promise, and we will—*soon*."

Most likely to be seen: Doing four things at once, all badly.

8. Normcore Norman

The most common sight on the playground, *Normcore Norman*, in his plain grey T-shirt, turtle-rimmed round glasses, and short brown hair of no recognisable style, is an everyman. You've spent dozens of hours together and yet you remember only that he does… something something product management? He's a vanilla human, a margherita man. You think his real name is Jim… no… John… no… James? There's a vowel in it, you're sure. With him, you small talk, pushing each conversation up a steep hill of banality and fake chumminess. The weather crops up often, as do the events of the previous weekend and the plans for the next. He finds almost everything you say to be "great", "awesome", and "brilliant".

His kid is Tim… no… Tom…. no… Tony? Something that doesn't grab attention. Something he picked from the top-ten-names list; the list everyone else avoided. His son watches the most popular shows and arrives at the playground clothed in the most popular, omnipresent children's brands. Paws that patrol.

Having a child wasn't a question for *Normcore Norman*,

nothing he agonised long and hard over. Everyone else was doing it, so he did it, too—he and the girlfriend he's been with since he was sixteen. So far, he has no strong opinions about the experience, or, best you can ascertain, anything at all. You realise—as you ask again about his plans for the weekend and agree that the forecast looks decent—that in the past year, you've laughed more with his two-year-old than with him; and that the kid has sharper insight about the world, too.

Of all the men featured in this list, *Normcore Norman* is the one you really hope other men don't see you as.

Catchphrase: None.

Most likely to be seen: Even if he's seen, he's instantly forgotten.

Be the Questioner You Would Want to Be Questioned By

As you sit around the edges of the playground, you might notice that someone has decreed that because you all have small people, the conversation must be similarly sized. That —just because you're tired, hungry, and sad, it's four hours until your parenting shift ends, your back hurts, and you've got a piece of spaghetti stuck to your ear—you can only ask each other questions such as "So how old is she, then?" or "Are they in kindergarten already?"

Fight it, Papa Bear!

Make your questions as piercing as your infant's hazel eyes. Go deep. Go hard. Stroke the shaft of controversy. Here are ten more meaningful questions you could ask, questions that will help you better understand, emphasise and entertain each other.

1. What has most surprised you about how you parent?

2. What's one thing you *want* to tell people about how you parent, and one thing you *don't* want to tell them?

3. How much has being a parent become part of your identity? Do you still feel like the old you when you're with your child? What about when you're away from them?

4. What are you doing differently from how your parents raised you?

5. How often did your parents say "I love you" and will you/are you saying it more or less? Why?

6. If you have a second child, do you want their personality to differ from that of your firstborn? If so, in what ways?

7. Where do you fall on the nature vs nurture divide? How much has that changed since you became a dad?

8. If you had to either double or half the speed of your child's ageing for the next year, which would you pick, and why?

9. Do you ever regret the decision to procreate?

10. Why didn't you tell me earlier that I had a piece of spaghetti stuck to my ear?

Envy

Sometimes when you're on the playground, you do something despicable, don't you?

Your eye roams. You don't mean for it to. Don't want it to. You're loyal, would never cheat or stray, you're not that type, and yet... you have scandalous, unfaithful thoughts, don't you?

Yes, you do.

You look at other children on the playground and you think, That one's better than mine. It's premium, while mine is a dented tin. A discount child. A bargain-bin baby. Look how that object of my fleeting parental desire is more symmetrical/has luscious, thick chestnut hair/already sleeps through the night/sits/stands/eats solids/walks/talks/poops in a potty etc., etc.

Yes, it's easy to covet. To play one child off against another, like Top Trumps.

Don't do that.

You can't swap. And anyway, your analysis is flawed. You can see only a few superficial traits. You don't know their full package, their many annoying hidden quirks. Some children are funny but neurotic. Others calm but dull. Some phases are easy, some are hard. Easy babies can become nightmare toddlers. Amazing toddlers become know-all, precocious kids. Pleasant six-year-olds become obnoxious preteens. Even the most loved can, for a time, become the most lost. The gifted still sometimes end up in the gutter.

This isn't a contest.

There are no prizes.

There isn't even an audience.

There is just you (flawed) and your child (flawed), wedded through genetics. Both trying to find meaning in the indifferent universe you were forced into, against your will, and for which the only suitable apology is being unconditionally loved—you by your parents and your child by you—with ferocious intensity, forsaking all others, in good phases and bad, until death do you part.

"You're Such a Good Dad."

I was at the playground. Of course I was at the playground. I was always at the playground. I threw Runa up in the air and she giggled. Near us was the half-empty jar of baby food—pumpkin and sweet potato—that I'd just finished feeding her. Less than 40 percent of it had made it into her mouth. I put her down and she crawled up the stairs to the slide.

I hovered behind her the whole way, just in case. I hadn't got used to her sudden jump in mobility. On her knees, she made it up, and at the top, she plonked her diapered butt down, holding up a conga line of rapidly annoyed toddlers now ascending the stairs behind her. I went round to the bottom of the slide and clucked like a chicken, flapping my arms to excite her down.

After a few moments, maybe a minute, an eternity for that jam of toddlers, she whooshed down. I grabbed her before she tumbled off and schnitzelled herself in the sand.

"You're such a good dad," said a nearby grandmother, at the playground with her granddaughter, Hanna, a regular (often snot nosed).

I turned. Yes, she was talking to me. This was the third

time this week that a woman had said something like this to me. Always while I'd been doing very normal, very banal, very everyday acts of public parenting.

"Thanks," I said, but what I actually thought was... Really?! Is this all it takes to be a good dad? Being on a playground? Clucking like a chicken? Catching my child at the end of a slide before they become a schnitzel? Is this how low the expectations of my sex are?

That's... sad.

And, to tell you the truth, kind-stranger lady, I don't even know if I am a good dad. I know I'm here, yes, although more in body than mind. I'm often parenting more in body than mind.

What I do know, of what I can be absolutely certain, is that Evelyn bought/stole/swapped/magicked the clothes my daughter is wearing—now smeared with a layer of pumpkin and sweet potato—into existence. In fact, every time I open the drawers in our apartment, there are new outfits. The hair on my daughter's head? Evelyn cuts it. The injections she got last week? Evelyn arranged them. The apartment where we sleep at night and shelter from the cold? Evelyn pays its rent. The two streets between here and said apartment, neatly paved, full of essential council services running above and below ground—her very high taxes help fund them. In fact, she's working right now, while I'm here, impersonating a chicken at the bottom of a slide.

Great fathering is almost always the result of great, multigenerational mothering. Of which I was a fortunate recipient. I hope, in the future, things will even out, but I don't think they have yet. Until then, we don't need praise. Women do.

Sex

You've just left a papa-child meet up. It's a Saturday morning and the midday nap looms large—two golden hours of peace, you hope. Your child is already powering down in the bike seat, pulling on his ears and sucking happily on his dummy. You need to get him home so he can nap because it's Saturday and his mum has had a few hours of peace this morning and he slept through last night and that means... well... might mean???

"Do you want to come to ours?" your friend Ian says, cradling his own child, four months older than yours. Already walking. "Put the kids down together for their nap?"

"Can't," you say. "I have to go home."

"Why?" he asks.

"This is the only weekly sex window we have," you say, a little embarrassed.

His eyes narrow. "You're going to have sex?"

"I didn't say that. Wouldn't be so casually presumptuous. I should have said that this is the only *possible* weekly sex window."

"What are the odds?" he asks.

You run the math; it's not pretty. "Five percent?"

He nods, seems impressed. "Yeah, you should go home."

You clip on your son's helmet. It has bunny ears. "Do you still have sex?" you ask Ian.

He laughs, and that's the answer.

Everyone warned you that you wouldn't have sex after you had children, and yet, like every other couple on earth, you and your partner thought, Naaaaah, we'll be the ones to prove them wrong.

Then you didn't prove them wrong, did you?

Naaaaah.

It's not that her body has changed. That's irrelevant. It's that *everything* has changed. Sex, you now realise, is a luxury good, and you two live in a time of relationship poverty: in a dry and dusty affection desert.

Sex won't keep your child alive. Sex won't make your child thrive. Sex will do nothing at all for your child, might even accidentally make another child, doubling or more likely tripling (quadrupling?) your existing problems.

So it's no surprise sex always finds itself at the bottom of the list, if it makes it onto the list at all because, really, who has the time to make lists?

It didn't used to be this way, of course. Before children, sex was simply the best way to fill an hour. One of life's few completely downside-less activities. Merely the inevitable conclusion of the two of you being in the same room for more than an hour. It was such fun you'd sometimes do it twice in a day because, well, why not? What better way was there to connect and expend all your excess energy? Remember excess energy?

Now, for you to have sex—in your touched-out, tired-out, tasked-out states—six different, very unlikely things need to have happened. You both need to have had at least five minutes of bodily autonomy that day, slept through the previous night, eaten something other than toast that week, touched each other that fortnight, had a conversation not about your child that month, and showered that quarter. You also need to find a large surface area not covered in dried puke, Lego firemen, or decapitated gummy bears.

Oh, and the kid needs to nap. The bloody kid better nap.

You climb onto the bike. It wobbles beneath you.

"I'd take a peck on the cheek," Ian says. "At this point."

"A cuddle would be nice," you say.

"Do people actually have sex?" he asks. Your kid is leaning precariously to one side like a famous tower in Italy. "I mean, I know I must have had it once, but it seems kind of..." He screws his face up. "Like getting a face tattoo, you know? Like... it's an option. It's a thing some people obviously do. But, also, it's kind of ludicrous. Know what I mean?"

"Yeah," you say, mentally trying to remember the last time you and your partner had sex. It's hard not to look at your child and conclude that it's the answer to the question your sexual attraction to each other once posed. You don't know if this is true, you certainly don't want it to be true—you just suspect it might be.

That's a question for a later time. Now, others matter more. Questions like: What shall we do for lunch? How should we fill the afternoon? How can we make more time for your spluttering career? When can we carve a window to visit the grandparents because they keep asking? How will we be as gentle to each other as we can, so we make it through the next year? How did we make such a great, funny kid? Did you hear what he just said? Did you see what he just did? He's glorious. We're glorious. This is glorious. I'm so attracted to this. To us. To our family.

You say goodbye to Ian and race home, chasing this fanciful, distant, ludicrous thing. You're not giving up. Not yet.

Five percent? You can work with that.

Good Night

Another frigid week passes and then you're in bed, lying side by side. You are the Scrollers, and the algorithm has you in its clutches, dousing you with just enough dopamine to seduce but not enough to sate.

Until... you do it. Somehow. You break free, lower your device, and slide next to her.

"What you doing?" she says.

"Giving you some fuss," you say, stroking her upper arm.

"Why, though?"

"What do you mean *why, though?*"

She looks at you and her forehead wrinkles. You see scenarios being modelled and their consequences being calculated. "Okay," she says, and lowers her phone, deciding she'll go with this, whatever it is. She turns onto her side. Your eyes meet. You are both free. You are out. You are offline. Your child is asleep. You are lovers, notionally. You pull her closer and kiss her mouth. Your hand reaches down and caresses her leg. You kiss for a while, and it is joyous. Time tap-dances. You become not one but definitely less than two. One and three-quarters? One and a half?

Until... "You're trying to have sex with me," she says.

You release your grip on her thigh. "I'm not."

"You're doing your moves."

"I'm not doing my moves. I don't have moves."

"I can't just switch it on. I know you can. That men can," she says, rounding up violently.

"And even if I did have moves—"

"I mean," she says, "when did we last kiss?"

"There's nothing wrong with wanting to have sex with your partner, which I'm not saying I'm trying to do. Or want."

"I don't think we touched each other in the past week."

You punch the mattress. The mattress is foam. Absorbs your punch, the mattress. Doesn't even feel it. "Any time I touch you, you accuse me of trying to have sex with you," you say. Your child murmurs in the next room. You both freeze. Panic fills you all the way to your top. Please, no more, you think. It is over, this day. We did it already. It is done.

Silence.

The kid was probably just turning over. Or having a dream. You relax and return to each other, no longer touching but at least looking into each other's eyes.

"So, if I wanted to have sex now, you wouldn't want to?"

"That's not..."

She sits up and removes her top. "Okay, let's have sex."

Your eyebrows plunge. It's a trick, you're sure. "Really?"

"Yeah."

You lunge for her. She pulls back. "See! I told you."

"Just because I'm willing to have sex doesn't mean I was *trying* to have sex!" you shout.

"I'm too tired to have sex."

"But you took your top off now. You can't toy with someone like that. That's... cruel."

Silence.

"At least put your top back on, then."

"Fine," she says, and does so.

More silence.

She rolls onto her back. She will soon pick up her phone and be lost to you.

"Blow job then?" you ask, valiantly.

She pulls in her lips. "No. Sorry."

Her hand reaches for her phone, next to her. The sheet you have washed the last four times. She pushes a button, the screen lights up. You're on ice. It's melting.

"Hand job?" you whisper. She sighs but releases her grip on the phone and turns to you. "I just find them so sad."

"Sadder than nothing?" you protest.

She mimes pumping a penis with her hand. "So mechanical, you know? Like an afternoon on the farm."

"Are they sadder than this conversation?"

She pats you on the stomach and picks up her phone. It's over. You have lost her.

Your teeth clench. You do so much for her and your family. You're being taken advantage of. You wish you were being taken advantage of. She's watching something funny and chuckles.

Life is chuckling at you too, and you know it. You're a sap. A patsy. A stooge.

It goes silent.

You consider, briefly, cutting her with really, really sharp words. Just cleaving into her. Ruining what little is left of this day and badly injuring tomorrow, too. Phrases come. You could do it. You know her weak spots. You resist.

More silence.

Another funny video. She chuckles.

"Good night," she says, thirty minutes later, without turning around.

The second part is true, you think, as you close your eyes.

The Fork Incident

It was a day like so many before it. The sun was in the sky, or thereabouts, and its position confirmed a precise configuration of hours, minutes, and seconds that everyone broadly agreed with. It was a Saturday, and we were in our apartment sitting in our extremely new, expensive, custom-built kitchen, just one week old.

Runa was crawling down the long, low shelf, perhaps seventy centimetres from the floor. She was pulling up on things and babbling nonstop now. The shelf ran all the way along the wall beneath the kitchen window; extra seating for when we had guests. Also, because, while we had a baby when designing it, we couldn't help fantasising about life with a toddler, and beyond that, with a child. We pictured Runa, pigtailed, quiet but self-assured, bookish and already conversational in Mandarin, aged perhaps six or seven, standing at the end of that low shelf and reaching up to the countertop, tiny, age-appropriate knife in her hands, helping us cut carrots while asking pertinent questions about why ras el hanout was the right spice for ragout.

We loved this long shelf. *Such a good idea.*

Runa crawled along the shelf towards me. "Waaahh-hawaashahhhhbabbabbababba," she said, astutely. She had a baby fork in her hands. She hit it against things as she moved and was having a thoroughly agreeable time.

Evelyn and I were sitting on either side of the table that abutted that long shelf, shovelling vegan schnitzel into our mouths. Like all parents, we ate as if we were in a speed-eating contest, never knowing how long it would be until the next interruption. Actually, Runa interrupted us so often that the times we weren't interrupted, when she didn't need something from us, had become the interruption.

Runa tried to pull herself up onto the windowsill. "Nein, Runa," Evelyn said, and prised her away, back onto the shelf. Runa sat, momentarily thwarted, and then said, "Aye aye," which, Evelyn told me, is what German children say when they stroke dogs. Runa adored dogs. "Aye aye" was her first word.

It was almost her first birthday. I shovelled in some more fake meat. Everything was beautifully, epically normal. In short, rushed, disjointed sentences, Evelyn and I tried to discuss a podcast we'd listened to the previous evening, which had detailed a tragedy: a child had fallen from a fifth-floor balcony and died. We hadn't meant to listen to it. Could no longer consume such stories. But it had been tacked onto the end of something else. We were discussing if we'd recover if something happened to Runa—coding our language, of course, not that she was old enough to under-stand the topic.

"I think I would be okay, eventually," I said. "Like, I'd be able to function. To feel human happiness again."

Runa gripped the table, lowered her head beneath it, and then popped back up. "Aye aye."

"Hello, hunny," Evelyn said, then turned back to me. "No, you wouldn't."

"Aye aye," Runa said, crawling off towards the collection of oat milks at the end of the long shelf, bashing her fork against the table.

"I've lived 95 percent of my life without YOU KNOW WHO, without being a P-A-P-A. I'd just go back to that."

Runa pushed on a carton of stacked milk. "Aye aye," she said.

"Don't push the milk, please," I said. "You know what, I'd run away. I'd move to Nepal and become like a, well, I don't know, what do they do in Nepal?"

"Monk, I guess?" Evelyn said.

"Aye aye," said Runa.

"I'm not monking. I'd become a gangster. Yeah, I'd go become a gangster in Nepal. But, like a nice gangster. On YouTube."

"Woof," Runa said, sitting down. "Woof. Aye aye. Oink oink."

"Yes, we did see a pig at the petting zoo yesterday," Evelyn said, then shifted out of her child-affirmation voice. "A YouTube gangster in Nepal?"

"Right. *Right.* Just like, you know, making videos about gangster life and stuff. I've got a harem. I'm doing whatever I want. F-U-C-K-I-N-G, mostly."

"Am I there?" Evelyn asked.

Runa tried to climb down. I helped her. "No," I said. "You'd remind me of her." I waggled my finger between us. "This is done. We're done."

"Oh," she says. "Right."

"It'd be fine, I think," I said. "After like a year or so. Because YOU KNOW WHO is not like an actual person, is she? She's more like a… penguin."

Runa climbed back onto the shelf. "Aye aye."

"No," Evelyn said. "I wouldn't get over it. I'd just walk around like I'd been shot in the face. With this big open wound, and everyone would see it, and yet they'd wouldn't want to ask about it because I'd break down. The wound would turn septic. My life would be ruined. Our relationship would be ruined."

"Well, I'm in Nepal, so."

A thud.

A cry.

Another thud.

A louder, more urgent cry.

Third thud.

PIERCING SCREAM.

HEART-STOPPING, WORLD-ENDING WAIL.

I span around and found Runa lying face down on the floor in the small gap between the back of my chair and the bank of kitchen drawers. Sickeningly, I realised the thuds had been made by her head as she fell off the end of that stupid, idiotic shelf. Those thuds had been made my child's head. Bouncing. Drawer. Chair. Drawer. Floor. Her one head. The container in which her only brain swam. The brain upon which everything meaningful in her life depended. There was blood too, from the fork. She'd forked herself in the face.

AND IT WAS ALL OUR FAULT.

We'd paid lab-people five thousand euros to IVF her here, this wonderful tiny penguin person with her wonderful mini limbs and her wonderful oversized eyes and her contextually inappropriate "aye ayes", and then we'd paid a kitchen-maker-man many thousands of euros to build this idiotic custom kitchen with its stupid, low, future-fantasy shelf from which Runa had tumbled, forking her own face out.

And I knew, knew that every time I looked at that shelf from now on, I'd remember this moment.

BECAUSE IT WAS ALL OUR FAULT.

Our neglect and our oversight and our basic, general,

everyday, run-of-the-fucking-mill inattentiveness had scarred our only child's only face for all eternity. And we were going to have to live with that, somehow. She was going to have to live with it too. And this was only the first one. The first time. The first scar.

Yes, we could be more vigilant.

Yes, we could hide the forks.

Yes, we could block that idiotic shelf.

Get down, we could say.

Stop.

Don't do that.

It's dangerous.

But it wouldn't matter. They were coming—the thuds and the scars. And it sucked. And this was parenting. And it would never end.

And all this knowledge arrived, at once, in that frozen fraction of a second with her there, face to the floor, motionless.

It was a lot.

It was too much.

It was not the most surprising thing.

For these insights surged up within me on a great, gushing geyser of love that knocked me forwards and down to her. I scooped her up and, in my arms, she cried like she'd never cried before, like the life was draining from her. We put on our shoes. Evelyn threw things in a bag. I started to order a taxi. Then we remembered some words of wisdom we'd heard: Every time your first kid is hurt, you go to the hospital. Every time your second is hurt, you bandage them up and take them to the doctor the next day. When your third is hurt, you pick them up, pat them down, and ask them what they want for dinner. It was a nasty fall, yes, but not a high fall. We waited. Runa cried herself into an exhausted sleep. The fifteen jagged minutes that took were the worst of my entire life. Worse even than the night of her birth. The wound, five centimetres below her eye, stopped bleeding long enough for us to see that it was deep, probably would be a scar, but that it was small.

The love kept flowing, long after it had already drowned me. Where was it coming from, all this love? How could there be so much of it? How had I not felt it before?

I'd suppressed it, I realised, the totality of the love I felt for my child. Had to. There was just no space for it. There was too much to do. So many daily tasks, chores, and obligations. The child needed to eat, sleep, be entertained, coaxed into her carrier, coaxed into the buggy, coaxed into the car, coaxed into sleep. I needed to buy nappies. I needed to call so-and-so about the thing. I needed to function, so I needed to suppress.

I'd suppressed it so well I hadn't even known how much was down there. It had taken a moment like this to release it. I wanted to puke. She stayed sleeping in my arms. Evelyn and I sat next to each other on the couch, both of us sobbing, unable to take our eyes off her.

"It's terrifying how much I love her," I said, eventually. "I'm so wrong. If something happens to her, we're fucked."

Evelyn nodded. "I know. I've always known."

Kindergarten

Runa was nearing one, somehow, and close to walking. With her birthday, a new, exciting option emerged—kindergarten (In Germany, Kindergarten is from age 3 to 6 or 1 to 6 if they also have a creche, like almost all of them in Berlin). Evelyn's mother was a lifelong kindergarten teacher, so we'd always known, in theory, that childcare options existed. That there were places where you could store your child while you did other, more economically fruitful things, or merely slacked off. We also knew that in Berlin, these child-storage facilities were free, basically.

We talked of it often, albeit vaguely.

"We should really apply to some kindergartens."

"Just six months until she's one, and you know what that means..."

"Kindergarten is coming."

It was like the mythical winter in *Game of Thrones*, only joyous, and so more of a *summer is coming*. Runa was an August birth, so she'd be eligible to start right after her first birthday. If we wanted that. Did we want that?

The playground was abuzz with kindergarten chatter:

Whose kids had started already? How was it going? For some families, the adjustment process took mere days; for others, it would take months—months before the parents could leave their children without said children becoming so distraught by the Industrial Baby Complex that the parents were called back to collect them.

We should have been excited about it, yet we weren't. I felt numb to the idea. I just couldn't imagine it. Runa was a pandemic baby. Our nearest family member lived seven hours away. In her entire life, she'd never been away from us. Never been cared for by anyone but us.

We'd never had a day off.

A night off.

Not one.

Not ever.

One of us was always there, with her, on duty. Still, we applied to some kindergartens, and a nice one replied. We went to meet their administrator. Evelyn and I sat in a small office, side by side, Runa on my lap, climbing me like a tree, as usual. She liked to climb my front and sit up on my shoulder, our faces almost touching. It made it difficult to maintain a conversation. I pulled her down.

We discussed the warming-up period. How it should be done by only one parent, they said. And it tended to be the fathers because the mothers had a hard time letting their children go. Often, they cautioned, the process was more traumatic for the parent than the child.

I agreed to do it. Starting the following Monday, Runa and I would come for an hour each morning. The week after that, if they felt Runa was ready, I'd leave for thirty minutes.

Then an hour.

Then for the whole morning.

Then, eventually, for the whole morning and part of the afternoon?!

I nodded while all this was being discussed, but I didn't believe any of it. It was as if someone were promising me a third arm. I didn't necessarily *not* want a third arm. I could imagine how it would be handy for, like, juggling and stuff, but I just didn't believe these people had a third arm to give, that it was the sort of thing one could offer someone else. I'd always had two arms, and I'd always had Runa, right there, in my face, trying to pull off my glasses, blowing raspberries on my cheeks, slapping my bald head, jumping up and down in my lap, climbing me like a tree.

I couldn't imagine not having that.

Until... a week into our daily one-hour visits. I was happily goofing around on the carpet, building with bricks. Runa was next to me, playing with a witch puppet, when her primary carer, Elif, said, "You can leave now."

I carried on playing because they were talking to someone else.

"Mr Fletcher, you can leave."

Fletcher was a common name.

"Let's try a few minutes, okay?"

"Hmm?" I said, looking up from what was rapidly becoming a modest but comfortable bedsit for the witch puppet.

"You can leave."

"Oh? Right. O-kay," I said, standing up, holding onto the couch as I did so, for the world was spinning at great velocity. Runa looked up at me, similarly confused. Why was I getting up? The witch's house had only half a roof. It wasn't near weatherproof. I bent back down and kissed her on the forehead, told her I'd come back soon. She narrowed her eyes, more confused than scared, perhaps expecting her mother to appear from the other door, tag-teamed in as usual; shift change.

"Have fun," I said, taking the first step away.

Her expression cracked and her lips trembled. *There is a natural order to things, and it's being upset. Why?*

Feeling a small but non-fatal tear in my heart, I hurried to the door of the kindergarten without looking back or breathing, yanked on the handle, and rushed out to the street.

The door closed behind me. I'd crossed a portal. There was no ceremony. No fanfare. Just a single, sharp transition. I'd been parenting // I was no longer parenting. I was outside, alone. The sun, in all its late-August strength, seemed to shine just for me. Birds bathed me in song. I took a deep breath. I began to walk and found my steps bouncy and light. The urge to whistle overpowered me.

I whistled.

I checked and... nope... no one wanted anything from me. I felt so light I might blow away. Not that there was any wind.

It was real.

It was true.

It was magical.

MY CHILD WAS SOMEONE ELSE'S PROBLEM.

Kindergarten! A third parent had entered our lives and was willing to do a nine-to-three shift every single weekday. That was a hell of a shift, nine to three. With it, Evelyn and I would get a substantial chunk of our old lives back.

Was that what I wanted? I probed but found I had no wants. The question had been irrelevant for so long, I no longer even knew what I could want. Like, what were desire's options?

I searched myself for feelings of guilt. Parents are so used to guilt; we do guilt better than we do choice.

Nope, I had no guilt either. Runa needed this. A new world to explore. No longer would she be forced to hang out all day with her lame-o parents. She'd be with other kids, navigating new social experiences. She'd get to inhabit a world that we didn't know about, away from us. That was a necessary step. A wonderful development. And it had to mean she was a human being, separate and autonomous, and not a... penguin. This realisation was startling. I grabbed a nearby lamppost to steady myself, bent forward, and took some deep breaths. When the dizziness passed, I stumbled into a coffee shop. Coffee was a thing people seemed to want. I thought maybe I could want it too?

"What would you like?" the heavily pierced lady asked.

I stared at the menu. I didn't know what I wanted. And I had so much time to decide. No one was hanging off me. Harassing and haranguing me. I found the menu bewildering. I felt like someone who'd been in a cult for decades and had been let loose in a McDonald's.

I ordered a cappuccino and was so giddy that I didn't even swear or throw something when the heavily pierced lady told me the price.

A woman entered behind me. Her name was Pauline. I'd seen her at the open day the kindergarten had hosted. Her child, Yma, had just started too.

"Hi," she said.

"Hi."

"Pauline."

"Adam."

"I have a confession," she said.

"Oh?" It seemed too early in our nascent relationship for confessions. "You're probably not going to remember this, but, when Runa was a newborn, you were in the supermarket. She was crying at the checkout. I told you she'd lost a sock."

Kind Eyes. My own flicked left, then right. Of course I remembered. I was still occasionally ranting about that day.

About all those women. The clucking mother hens and their unsolicited advice.

Sockgate, I now called the incident. It had earned a *gate*.

"Vaguely," I said.

"It was me," she said, smiling guiltily.

"How do *you* even remember that?" I asked. "It was like ten months ago?"

"Because you were so pissed," she said.

We laughed for a long time. "You did the right thing," I said, and maybe believed.

"Did I?"

"I'm not good at taking advice."

She nodded. My pocket vibrated. I pulled out my phone. It was the kindergarten.

"She's inconsolable," Elif said. "Come back."

I looked at my watch. Seven minutes had passed. "I have to go," I told the heavily pierced lady, as the milk frother hissed and steamed in the background.

"Do you want it togo?" she asked, because in Germany they've adopted the English phrase "to go" but mash the pronunciation, so it sounds like the name of a country in West Africa.

"I won't have enough hands," I said. If Runa was crying, she'd demand to be picked up. She was heavy now. I'd need two hands just for her. I really did need three arms… "And I have to go right now. I'm needed."

"So, what then?" she asked.

"I'll come back for it."

I returned to the kindergarten, where I was handed a tight ball of despair. I consoled it while carrying it against my chest all the way back to my coffee togo, waiting on the counter. Pauline had togo-ed too, and was gone.

Runa and I sat together by the window. "Good day at kindergarten?" I asked, wiping a tear from her eye, just above her scar, just above the spot where she'd loved to be stroked as a baby. She smiled and then reached up and tried to slap me on the head.

"Aye aye," she said, and I realised these weren't slaps— they were attempted strokes.

"Yeah," I said. "I had a great day, too. And tomorrow's going to be even better."

Birthday Party

"Ha-pppy biiiiiiiirthday dear Runa. Ha-pppy.... biiiiiiiirthday to you."

The crowd broke into cheers. Runa was standing on the bench in the corner of the beer garden, leaning on the table for support, a giant inflatable balloon with a 1 on it over her head, shyly enjoying the attention of her birthday.

I started cutting her unicorn cake. This was it. We had done it. An entire year. We were a month late celebrating, but she didn't know that. We'd wanted to do it earlier, but with so many people away in August, and with kindergarten starting, we'd decided to wait.

I handed around slices of cake to our friends and their kids, many around her age. This was the day we'd counted down to.

You're only in the trenches for the first year.

I became so distracted slicing cake that when I next looked up, Runa had crawled off somewhere. This wasn't like her. She never wandered off. Was never more than thirty centimetres from her mother or me, as if tied by an invisible string.

Kindergarten was shifting something.

I looked around for Runa because I was always looking around for Runa because that was my job. I didn't find her, but I found Evelyn, also scanning for Runa. We were a team. We would remain a team. We were also a couple, just about. And a family: a happy, functional family.

It was worth the work. Worth the sacrifice.

Evelyn smiled. There was no Divide between us anymore. I had met the goal I'd set myself in the taxi ride to the hospital, some thirteen months ago. *Mama* and *Papa* were meaningless labels to Runa—we were interchangeable, and this filled me with pride.

I spotted her. Runa and Yma, her friend from kindergarten, were stickering each other on the dance floor. Yma was all we ever heard about. Yma was her world when we were not her world. We knew little about that world, as she didn't have enough words yet to describe it. But she could say "Yma", sort of, just about.

The music grew louder. There were cheers and shouts. Runa was oblivious to where we were and what we were doing. That had never happened before. It was gigantic. The tectonic plates of our lives were reshaping themselves beneath our feet.

I walked to Evelyn. "This is weird."

"This is weird," she agreed.

"What do we do?"

"Dance?" she suggested.

"I'll just get her," I said.

"Leave her."

I squeezed through the crowd towards Teddy, Yma's father, who was supervising the girls. He had Yma in his arms, was twirling her around. Pauline was there too. Runa held up her hands to her, asking to be picked up. I butted in and reached down for her, but she pushed my hands away. She wanted to be held by Pauline, not me.

"I can take her," Pauline said, shooing me away and scooping her up.

She'd never preferred anyone to us.

I thought back to the miserable years of IVF and pregnancy; to the endless ordeal that was birth; to the sleepless nights, the sleep regressions, the bellyaches, the time when Runa was hospitalised for a week because she kept losing weight; to all the times we'd co-suffered, all the games of Baby Blackjack I'd lost; to the fork incident; and to all the delicious firsts. So many firsts.

And now, another one—wilful independence.

"I'm proud of us," I said, as I reached for Evelyn's hips and pulled her into me.

"Me too," she said, looking over her shoulder. "And of her. Watching her, I have this really intense nostalgia. Do you know what I mean?"

"No."

She dug deeper. "I think having a kid completes the life cycle, somehow. It's the closest you can get to re-experiencing your childhood—the childhood you no longer remember."

"I like that," I shouted, over the song's trumpet. "I'm going to steal that for my book."

"You always steal my ideas."

"I know."

"Will you credit me?"

"Probably not, no."

"Are you definitely writing a parenting book?"

"I think so. I was going to wait until she was two, but I'm already forgetting so much. I don't want to forget it. I don't know if I want to come out of the trenches."

Evelyn frowned. "Me neither."

We kept dancing, trying to distract ourselves from how this didn't feel like we'd thought it would feel. We failed.

In the gap between songs, I leaned into Evelyn. "We could always have another one?" I said.

"Fuck off."

———

(Not) The End

Writing this book (and its predecessor on pregnancy and birth) has been a very emotional, cathartic experience. Thank you for reading. Please consider leaving a review/rating, it really does help.

Want to know what happened next? I can't wait for you to meet two year Runa, she's a blast. Join me for a tour of the terrible/terrific toddler years in **Dad Differently: Toddlers** - the third book in the series.

It's available for pre-order and should be out in the first quarter of 2024. I hope to see you there.

Adam

Also by Adam Fletcher

Notes

8. Micromumming

1. Russell, J, et al (2001), *Brain preparations for maternity--adaptive changes in behavioral and neuroendocrine systems during pregnancy and lactation.* Progress in Brain Research 2001;133:1-38.
2. Hendrick, V, et al (1998), *Hormonal Changes in the Postpartum and Implications for Postpartum Depression*, Psychosomatics, Volume 39, Issue 2, 1998, Pages 93-101, ISSN 0033-3182,
    https://doi.org/10.1016/S0033-3182(98)71355-6.
3. Stickel, S, et al (2021), *Endocrine stress response in pregnancy and 12 weeks postpartum – Exploring risk factors for postpartum depression*, Psychoneuroendocrinology, Volume 125, 2021, 105122, ISSN 0306-4530,
    https://doi.org/10.1016/j.psyneuen.2020.105122.
4. Kumsta, R. Heinrichs, M (2013), *Oxytocin, stress and social behavior: neurogenetics of the human oxytocin system*, Curr. Opin. Neurobiol., 23 (1) (2013), pp. 11-16, 10.1016/j.conb.2012.09.004
5. Mogavero, M, et al. (2021) *Increased Serum Prolactin and Excessive Daytime Sleepiness: An Attempt of Proof-of-Concept Study.* Brain Sci. 2021;11(12):1574. Published 2021 Nov 28. doi:10.3390/brainsci11121574
6. Sobrinho, L. (1998), *Emotional aspects of hyperprolactinemia.* Psychother Psychosom. 1998;67(3):133-9. doi: 10.1159/000012273. PMID: 9667060.

13. The Breastapo, Part 2

1. Oster, E (2019). *Cribsheet: A Data-Driven Guide to Better, More Relaxed Parenting, from Birth to Preschool.* New York, Penguin Books.

15. Parenting Intelligence

1. 1936 February, Esquire, *The Crack-Up: A desolately frank document from one for whom the salt of life has lost its savor* by F. Scott Fitzgerald, Start Page 41, Quote Page 41, Column 1, Esquire Inc., Chicago, Illinois. (Esquire archive at classic.esquire.com)

18. Pacifiers

1. Hauck, F, et al (2005), *Do pacifiers reduce the risk of sudden infant death syndrome? A meta-analysis. Pediatrics.* 116: 716–23. DOI : 10.1542/peds.2004-2631.
2. Nowogrodzki, A. (2020). *How to Ditch the Pacifier.* The New York Times. https://www.nytimes.com/article/parenting-pacifier-guide.html.

29. Be Careful What Your Kid Wishes For

1. Tallis, F. (2018). *The Incurable Romantic: And other tales of madness and desire.* Little, Brown Book Group.

30. Sleep Regression

1. MNT. 2021. *What Are The Stages Of Sleep Regression?* Medical News Today. www.medicalnewstoday.com [Accessed October 2023]

34. Parenting Parity

1. This entry was inspired by the wonderful *Abbott Awaits: A Novel*, by Chris Bachelder.

35. Sleep Training

1. Mindell, J, et al (2006). *Behavioral treatment of bedtime problems and night wakings in infants and young children.* American Academy of Sleep Medicine. Oct;29 (10): 1263–76. Erratum in *Sleep*, Nov 1;29 (11):1380. PMID: 17068979.

Printed in Great Britain
by Amazon

43900842R00116